Dedicated to Jack and Kristen

My Vacuum Book

Vacuums, Vacuums in a row,
Vacuum, Vacuum watch them go!
Even though they scare me some,
When mommy starts it, watch me run.

Vacuums, Vacuums big and small,
Vacuum, Vacuum …I love them all!
Blue ones, black ones, even red
They eliminate fuzz balls under my bed.

They suck up dust that makes us cough.
And I do admire it when it's off.
This one looks like Mommy's and mine,
I think about them all the time.

--written by Mommy Perone
December 23, 1996

Contents

Introduction: About This Book

This book started as a short journal entry, a brief vignette after two glasses of wine and an argument with my husband. My husband Dave was criticizing me for being on the computer all the time. So finally we were having a discussion and the truth came out. He was worried about me. I asked him if he was 'worried about me', throwing my fingers up in air quotes, why didn't he just say so, again throwing my fingers up, rather than make fun of me on a daily basis with jibes such as "There you are again in the same spot you were in this morning—"

"Of course, that is the only way to grow roots," I interrupt in my head.

"—at the computer..."

Why do men use sarcasm to curb behavior, rather than just expressing concern? The latter will work 100% of the time, the former about 0%. Once I realized what he was worried about, I assured him I was not pulling away from society, as he feared. I was *writing.* Yes, writing. Not web surfing, not buying stuff on eBay, or Facebook-ing. *Writing.*

I am *writing.* I even joined a writing group the week before. The first class was approaching in a week. So we talked about that, too. It was just before Labor Day 2010.

Now, it all made sense. I understood the friction in our home. It was good to clear the air. I explained that there isn't money to be made by vacuuming, for goodness sake. I am planning a book on grief and just beginning to clear my head, a process I find therapeutic. The time was simply right to write.

I had begun transcribing my old journals, jotting down ideas, and putting my new concepts to paper. It wasn't always easy, but it was the right thing to do at the right time. I found my lighter side, able to express my humorous perspectives on life and would type them out as they came to me. So with the air cleared, I typed one up while Dave watched the Yankee game. It was about a funny episode with my mother, one of many. It was a vignette, you might say.

Two months earlier, I had resigned from my overwhelming public relations job, a drastic measure, but one that was necessary. I needed to spend more time with my thirteen-year-old son, who was failing school. Six months prior, I watched my sister die of cancer at thirty-four years old. The five years before that, well, let's just say those years were a journey, as you will see. I felt a push deep in my soul; a voice telling me to leave before I wrote a manifesto on the state of public relations and felt compelled to distribute it and flame publicly.

So *carpe diem* it was. It was time to take the lemons and make lemonade. I was drowning and needed to turn some of this pain into something positive. It was clearly time for me to focus on what was important in my life. But when you are operating so closely and in concert with your soul, it can be worrisome for your spouse. I do understand why Dave was worried about my change in behavior.

I spent a great deal of time thinking about why I wanted to quit my job. *Do I really need to make myself crazy giving my life over to work? Steve is failing school. He needs me and he's all I have. He will be leaving for college in five short years. Then I*

*can work 24/7. I want to spend time with my 2-year-old nephew
in Connecticut. The peace and quiet of a day of writing would be
good for me. I need to reassess and recover and this is the time.
I'm resigning and we are lucky we can afford it because we are
conservative. That is positive. All good.*

Beyond those logical reasons, my gut said, *"Now!"* It was
a strong message and I was ready to listen. So immediately after
resigning from my job, I began transcribing my old journals. It
wasn't easy to go back and read those passages, yet it was cathartic
and reminded me how much we had survived.

I was also shuttling my son back and forth to summer school,
taking him to all his appointments, doing family chores, paying
bills, and looking for areas where expenses could be cut. I knew
I was doing the right thing when all of Steven's doctors, dentists,
and orthodontists reacted to seeing me.

"Hi, haven't seen you in a while!" they all said.

"Yeah, it's been about two years." Since I started working
almost an hour away from home, Dave was in charge of all things
that happened in the early afternoon in our life. Dave has always
been great supporter of my work and husband who shares respon-
sibilities 50/50.

I was 41 and, in essence, climbing down the ladder. Surely,
there is a great deal of money saved by *not* living a frantic modern
lifestyle, I figured. In fact, I made a list. That too, would be a great
book. This is my year to live on the edge. Was it dangerous? Yes.
Dangerous to reduce to one income voluntarily during a recession,
dangerous because I am used to being a working woman, dangerous
because people may not understand, dangerous because I am breaking the norm. And yes, I did do *some* vacuuming, if not as much as
my husband expected. Let's just say I laid-off the cleaning lady.

So, after writing the vignette about a funny episode with my mother, I decided to share it with Dave. I turned the laptop toward him. "See, this is something I just whipped up."

He read it quietly, looked at me in all sincerity and said, "I don't get it."

I felt myself deflate. I thought it was a very funny memory.

A week later, I attended my first writing group. When my turn came to read, I chose to read that vignette. The group loved it. After their encouragement, I felt vindicated. Not everyone is your audience. I realized that if I was serious about writing, I must share my personal work with discretion, especially at this vulnerable beginning. I needed an audience of readers and writers, not a husband who reads one book a year at the beach. His response could have been influenced by a million reasons, beyond my ability to write. *(Note to aspiring writers: always get a second opinion.)*

I was practically in tears after hearing comments from the writing group:

"I love it when people talk about their mothers."

"The imagery you used made her real to us. You told us so much in such a short amount of text."

"It told us a lot about you, too."

"That is a very contemporary piece."

"Your mother is the matriarch presiding over the family resources – all the resources!"

"Your mother seems like someone we would have liked to know."

I perked up at the last comment. I replied, "Oh, she's still alive and well!" Thank God, I thought.

As I dabbed my eyes with a tissue, I was having one of those gigantic feeling waves. The kind of feeling that indicates that you are on to something big; the kind of feeling wave that occurs in your life only a handful of times. A dozen, if you are lucky. *Getting your dream job. Nailing the presentation. Giving birth!* I have had those three already, and for me, another very real moment in my life, a very real gigantic feeling wave, was the fact that this group 'got it.' They...got...it! I will be forever grateful to those wonderful people.

If I have piqued your interest, the vignette I am referring to is "My Eggs Over Easy"!

Since that time, the writing flowed from my soul and took me on a detour to humor. My mother was pleased. She worried that I would write dark and disturbing things, tragedy, basically what I like to read. My writing flowed like white river rapids. My fingers plucked away at each key like rain drops in a building downpour. The memories began coming to me faster and faster. *Drip drip ...drippedy drip, drippedydrippedy drip, whoosh, gush, gush, gurgle.*

There are laughs in this book. However, I am not making fun of my mother. The humor is not trite. To me, it reveals the powerful nature of our real human relationships. I adore my mother and her humor, *our shared humor,* which demonstrates her courage, spirit, and resilience. There are tears in this book. Life is hard and everyone has their own version of hard.

As you read, I hope you find familiar connections with your mother or other women in your life. I bet that you will 'get it.'

Enjoy!

Kim Perone

Vacuum like no one is watching

The whirr of the vacuum could be heard for hours each day wafting out the windows of 136 N. Toll Street in Scotia, New York, a little sandalwood-colored bungalow in a sleepy little suburb of Schenectady, the home of General Electric.

"Dad, does she sleep with that thing?"

I used to ask my father if Mom slept with the vacuum. She seemed in love with the vacuum. We joked and pictured her tucking it in at night. We had forest green sculpted wall-to-wall carpet and paneling from floor to ceiling. While Mom vacuumed, my sister and I picked the pills off our green, yellow and brown plaid sofa and chair.

My mother, Claudia, loves to clean. I mean, it makes her feel so good to bustle around her house, or anyone's house for that matter, vacuuming. And laundry? Don't get her started; she can't stop. I suspect she washes perfectly clean clothes just to keep the washer and dryer humming in unison with the vacuum.

Mom is a little tiny woman, 4 foot, 11 inches, with a short bob of bright blonde hair. All 110 pounds of her loves whirring around the house vacuuming – it doesn't even have to be her house. At my sister Kristen's house, during visits when Kristen would make a move to clean, I would say "Don't do that. What's Mom going to do when she gets here? Let's just enjoy our visit." Mom likes it more than we do. Neither of us got the clean-like-your-life-depends-on-it gene.

When Mom heard I had hired a cleaning lady, she was shocked that anyone paid for cleaning. Then she was doubly shocked at the price.

"I could do it for that!" she said.

"Mom, of course you could do it. People don't love to clean like you do." She was still shocked.

"She only cleans the common areas?" she would ask. "She moves the dishes out of the way to clean the sink, but doesn't actually clean them? What the heck?"

"Hey, I guess that's in the rule book or something."

I cleaned for the cleaning lady, actually. On the day of her arrival, I found myself running around like a mad woman in the morning, picking up piles of papers, dirty coffee cups, and yesterday's bath towels, so she can reach the surface area of our life. But it was all worth it. What a treat it was to start the weekend off with a mopped, dusted, and yes, vacuumed house with clean bathrooms.

After all, I was working a long hours. I was tired and coming home late. We were investing massive amounts of time at my son Steven's baseball games and frankly, that was where I should be on weekends. If I was working so hard, and being a Good Mom, surely I deserved a little domestic assistance.

Now I am a writer, so I let our cleaning lady go. In this instance, most people would feel the call of housework pulling them away from the computer, but not me. The computer calls me away from my housework. I don't want to stop writing and I certainly don't want to start vacuuming. Of course, Dave was teasing me about the time I spent on the computer. Imagining the worst of web surfing or even something nefarious, maybe espionage? Chat rooms?

"I write," I said. "I am used to sitting at a computer most of the day. I did a lot of that at my job. You just didn't see it. It is like me saying that you spend too much time on lawns." (My husband owns a lawn care company.)

"Well, I do spend too much time on lawns, I should be doing more managing and tracking from the office," he responds.

"Okay, yes, but you know what I mean."

The computer is where my work occurs, especially now. He said he just would like to see me "doing more."

Are you going to say it?

"I'd like to see you do more..."

Don't say it.

"Like..."

You are not going to say it, are you? "...cleaning."

Now, you've gone and said it.

"....vacuuming."

Dear God in heaven, do you even know me?!? Where am I going to hide the body?

On closer observation, I think I *am* scarred by growing up with the vacuum running all the time. I like what the vacuum does certainly, but I abhor its smell and sound. I always seem to run over the cord and bump into furniture legs. I lack patience. It fights me every step of the way. I wheeze in its presence. Dave constantly unplugs the clogs.

My reaction to the situation is to keep buying new vacuums. I like them before they become gummed up with our debris. Once they are sullied, I slink away, like an embarrassed friend. *Tomor-*

row. Tomorrow, I will vacuum. Yeah. I don't ever expect that feeling to go away.

So the title of this book is a dedication to my mother Claudia, her love, a love she passed on to me (the love part, not the love of vacuuming part). I know she wishes me the best in life. She wishes for me to vacuum like no one is watching, in careless abandon and joy. I picture her graceful pirouettes around an orange canister vacuum, human and machine moving in beautiful synchronicity. It is some sort of modern (or classic?) dance.

Little does she know, I *do* vacuum like no one is watching. I cough and sneeze and grunt and groan and clog and blog about how much the vacuum and I are enemies.

I hope no one is watching, because it sure isn't pretty.

Kim Perone

Didn't your mother teach you...?

On any given day, I am reminded of all my mother taught me; specifically those common sense lessons that teach you how to behave. By behave, I mean act in such a way that the world continues in a smooth, polite, and orderly manner. Whenever I see someone do something that breaks these behavior rules I think, *Didn't your mother teach you…?*

A great example of this is how to behave in public bathrooms. The world would be a better place if more mothers taught their daughters to put paper down over the seat rather than dangle and make a mess. Like my mother taught me. *Really.*

Or when my husband walks away after an argument grumbling about *me* under his breath within *my* range of hearing! I can hear you! Didn't your mother teach you not to do that? Mine did. That is a heinous crime. *Seriously.*

Then there are all of those other things, like closing the pizza box top to keep the heat in and the screen door to keep bugs out. Nothing irritated my mother more than glasses left all over the living room. We used coasters to protect the furniture. However, we always needed reminding.

"Pick that glass up!"

We also made a habit of cleaning our rooms every Saturday morning before we did anything fun. We never watched television past 10:00 AM on a Saturday or Sunday. One time I stayed overnight at my friend's house and was shocked to wake up in the morning and watch in awe as the whole family (minus their mom, who was cooking all the time) piled into the living room with their pillows, in their pajamas, proceeding to watch movies on pay channels all day long! It felt somehow dirty.

At our house, vacuuming was a daily chore, of course. I had a really hard time with that one, given my distaste for the vacuum, as you now know, but I did learn that it was a good thing to do. And despite my vacuum deficiency, I have a healthy respect for regular vacuuming.

I, for one, am forever grateful for all those little lessons from Mom and for all of those who occupy the same world who also learned them. I hope I can leave a lasting impression on my son in a significant way, but I also hope to give him the knowledge from those little lessons, the common sense behavior that makes him pleasant to be around. I am working really hard on this these days – teeth brushing, deodorant, flushing the toilet, taking shoes off before walking farther into the house. This knowledge is sure to make him subtly nice to be around, yet secretly annoyed when others break the rules. He too might think, *didn't your mother teach you?*

If not for being a mother myself, I would surely take for granted those little lessons that make me who I am. I would think I just *knew* what to do, think I was born with it, forgetting that my mother had to reinforce rules over the years. For people who have lost their mothers, or their mothers have lost themselves, my heart breaks. I cannot imagine how much harder it must be to learn these lessons. My nephew lost his mother to cancer at fifteen months old. My beautiful sister will not be able to teach Owen her special lessons. Although during his first year of life she did teach him a wonderful lesson – to eat his vegetables.

Kim Perone

As a vegetarian, she gave him spinach right out of the gate, and anything else green and out of the norm. Edamame, anyone? Now given that he only started eating solid food at eight months old, the seven-months-lasts-a-lifetime lesson is impressive. It is deeply imbedded in him now. We see it each time he eats the green items first. You would be surprised how funny it is to see a little kid spit out meat and gobble down asparagus! Mom and I promise to be there for Owen, in her stead, as any needs arise.

My friend Kay's mother left when she was five years old. Her mother was an alcoholic who evidently felt that it was better to leave than teach her children anything. Kay was the oldest of three girls. She raised her sisters. In the subsequent years, her father had two boys with two different women. He had his own problems, which included drug addiction. While he was serving a couple of years in jail, Kay and her husband gained custody of her little half-brother. Doesn't say much for his mom either, eh? When I think of what a wonderful mother my friend is, I ask myself how on earth she managed that!

These are the true overachievers, the unsung heroes, those who develop on their own, carefully observing the behaviors of others they want to emulate. Her guide must have been what her mother *didn't* teach her. Or better yet, she learned to do the opposite of what she saw, to want the opposite for her children.

For me, this is proof positive that there is a mother lesson for us all.

Kim Perone

My Mother, My Girl Scout Leader

My mother, the dynamo, the frustrated housewife, was my Brownie and Girl Scout leader. She painted our basement floor gray, adding a painted round Brownie circle with our troop number stenciled in yellow within it. Our Brownie meetings were held in the basement. We had a school-size blackboard down there, an item my father was able to get when he was working at a school during renovations. We could feel the cool concrete floor against our buttocks under the short Brownie skirts as we sat on the circle.

When I think back, my mother was the leader for everything. From homeroom mother to Girl Scout leader, she championed our programs with her energy and creativity. I remember making fortune cookies from scratch. Whatever Mom did, she did well.

However, my mother wasn't some sappy lovey-dovey mommy. She was quick to tell me that the second graders in my Brownie troop were much better behaved than me and my snotty third grade friends. She pointed out that I might be the ringleader for those sassy girls. I was probably just trying to be cool and feeling ownership over the group. After all, the meetings were held at my *own* house and my *own* mother was the queen. Doesn't that make me some sort of Brownie princess? Apparently not.

As we graduated from Brownies to Girl Scouts, Mom was again my leader. On a trip to Rollerama, the local roller skating arena, when I was returning my skates at the end of the day, I fainted. I was standing next to her and just a moment before said, "I am soooo tired."

While I was on the ground, she kicked me, "Get up, get up!" She thought I was being silly. When she turned me over and saw my eyes rolling back in my head, she realized I wasn't kidding. As she describes it, "All my first aid training went out the window because it was my own kid! I was screaming, 'Is there a doctor in the house?'" To this day, she feels guilty. I love that she feels guilty, not because she *should* but because it reinforces how much she loves me. You never outgrow that comfort.

I am lucky to have inherited my mother's leadership qualities. I am quick to jump in and lead any group. When I was fifteen, I was the captain of the junior varsity cheerleading squad. We were responsible for cheering with each other. The JV cheered from the stands with varsity for the varsity game, and vice versa.

"You say red, we say white, you say Tartans, we say fight!" clap clap clap, stomp stomp stomp.

During the JV game, they were messing with us and wrecked our cheer by hollering the wrong words. They decided to say "purple" and "brown" very loudly instead of "red" and "white" with us. I was furious. So, I organized a sit-in against the varsity cheerleaders, instructing my squad to refuse to cheer with them. We boycotted the varsity basketball game by sitting in a completely different area of the gym.

Ms. D, the cheerleading coach and school volunteer, didn't understand at all and I got in trouble. The punishment I do not recall, but do remember it was worth it. I was standing up—or rather sitting down—for what I believed in and leading my girls. That was more important than any punishment.

Kim Perone

When I think back, I should not have been a cheerleader at all. But I had no confidence in any other sport. I was overly curvy, clumsy, and slow. Cheering has become much more physical over the years, requiring a greater level of athleticism. But the stigma lingers. Dave teases me. "Kimmy was a *cheeeeerleader*," he says in a high-pitched voice.

To which I reply in the timeless words of Gwen Stefani, "Ain't no hollerback girl...." but I am not ashamed.

When it was time to go to college, the other mothers were pining away, "Oh, I am going to miss Susie so much," sniff, sniff.

My mother's famous line was, "Are you kidding? I can't wait for Kim to leave!" with an emphasis on can't and wait.

I was not a troublemaker, but if memory serves, we were too similar to live in the same house for much longer. (With the obvious exception of the clean-gene.) My mother would tell me what to do and I would argue about the principle of making my own decisions, such as cleaning my room (surprise, surprise). I should be able to make my own decisions. I am sure I was thinking, "It's better to leave the dust where it lies than to stir it all up, *duh*."

On the other hand, my sister would say "sure" then do whatever she wanted rather than what was asked of her. Many years later, Mom said she preferred that style. "Ignore me, but don't argue with me."

As a mom myself, I now see the wisdom in that approach, and Steve is more like Kristen. But honestly, I would relish a good, thought-provoking argument from Steven now and again, even "I want to clean my room on Fridays, not Saturdays," or "I am old enough to determine my own bedtime."

Mom says I was the classic firstborn, sociable, mature, open, and expressive. They used to say "Kimmy dance, Kimmy sing." Of course, I obliged. They look back now and say I was the "experimental child," realizing that there were some overreactions in parenting. My parents had tons of youthful angst and pent-up frustration to back up my groundings. My sister was shy and kept her thoughts to herself leading my parents to believe she was dark and disturbed, so they backed off tremendously. If she was going out with friends, they were just happy she was socializing. She was smart like that. She kept herself hidden and was not an open book, like *moi*.

Mom and Dad didn't put restrictions on her, such as a curfew. Whereas for *me,* my best friends from high school will tell you that my parents "photocopied our driver's licenses and performed background checks. Oh, and then we needed to bring her back by 10:30 PM."

When I was sixteen, my parents caught me smoking. It still sends shivers down my spine. Whenever I tell the story, I stress *"reg*-u-lar cigarettes, not funny ones." You would have thought the world had come to an end. I was grounded indefinitely! For most parents that would equal a month, for mine, however, it meant six months to a year and only then slowly earning back privileges.

The cheerleading tryouts for the following year were the day after I was caught. *Curses.* I was not allowed to try out. Explaining to all my friends why I didn't try out for the squad after all of the preparation was, obviously, humiliating. Today, I am still technically grounded. I guess Dave inherited the charge of the sentence. My son will ask, "You're still grounded, right, Mom?"

"Yep, I sure am," I say dryly.

Years later, as a young adult, I learned to respect their level of discipline, sharing the story with a friend who caught her teen

Kim Perone

smoking. She asked me, "Well, did it make you stop smoking?" and I realized it didn't.

"So you still had to come to your own decision?" she asked or, rather, pointed out wisely.

"Yes, I did," I replied. (And I did eventually quit.)

Kim Perone

Run Up the Hill...

"**R**un up the hill and get me a beer and Kleenex," Mom would always say. She had tissues around her all the time. Tissues were in every room of the house, in her purse, in her shirtsleeve. Allergies, I think. The hill she was referring to was the front lawn of camp; one hundred yards of steep, uneven turf and tightly-mowed weeds. From the sandy beach to the kitchen door, the elevation increased by thirty feet.

When I was eleven years old, Mom and Dad decided it was either time for another house with a bigger yard or a summer camp. A camp seemed a bit of a stretch, but it was 1980 and the real estate market was down. Lucky for us, it was a buyer's market. Driving around Sacandaga Lake on a Saturday in the fall, Dad turned down a dead end road and stumbled onto his paradise—a little green house with a rickety redwood deck and a hundred feet of sandy beachfront facing a calm cove. The dead end road was actually a peninsula that stretched out to a rocky point looking out toward the rest of the lake. *Sold!*

Our pre-camp days involved *real* camping, every weekend, rain or shine. By real, I mean tenting on the islands of Lake George. Mom and Dad would pack up the food, coolers, tent, and screened-in room and put it all in the boat. We drove the boat to our camp site on the island and unloaded. Mom and I had matching olive green sweatshirts with iron-on red fuzzy feet walking up the front of us. Mom's first job after we landed on terra firma—clean the outhouse. After Mom was done, it was spider-free, fresh-smelling, and the hole was topped with a toilet seat. All it needed was a vase with fake flowers in the corner and Grandma's embroidery framed and hung on the wall. It was the original *'posh potty.'*

I give my parents credit for the work they put into this summer activity. Each year Dave and I say we will take Steven tenting, but each year we get to the end of our busy summer, look at each other and say, "Nah, next year." None of us, including Steven, is really interested in camping. It is hard work. Steve has sports all summer, and frankly, we are too plugged into our modern conveniences. We can't do unplugged.

So when the camp was ours, we moved up there for the summer. We spent Memorial Day until Labor Day living at camp, leaving our bungalow in Scotia during the summer. Back at home, where the windows were about two feet from the neighbor's house, three teenage sisters were fighting. With the windows open you could hear them screaming a variety of female affronts.

"You took my shirt! Give it back."

"Maaahhhhommmmm. She hit me!"

"I hate you!"

"Bitch!"

But we were not there to hear it anymore! Ah, that was a major victory.

In Scotia, we had what they call a "postage stamp" yard which was alongside a driveway that could barely fit our boat and trailer. I remember my father's skillful jockeying of the car as he backed the boat and trailer into the driveway. My mother directed, "...left, a little more right, a little more left." The space left no room for even a blade of grass between the driveway and our house and the house next door. Camp was my parents' paradise.

Because we moved up for the summer before school ended, all four of us would wake up at 5:00 AM, get ready for work or school, and pile in the car with our dog, Charlie Brown, and drive to the house. We all met again for the trip back up to camp when Dad got home from work.

At camp, once summer was officially in full swing, cocktail hour was held on the dock starting precisely at 4:00 PM. It was adults-only. If we were on the dock when the whistle blew, my mother and her friend, Karen, would kick us off. It was the end of their stay-at-home-mom workday; the female version of the tavern around the corner from the manufacturing plant. During the day, both moms had worked hard doing laundry and vacuuming up the never-ending sand.

Mom would sit at the end of the dock to soak up the sun. We kids must have looked like we needed a job. "Run up the hill and get me a beer and a Kleenex," she would say. Much to Mom's chagrin, in our adulthood my sister Kristen and I would repeat this line and laugh.

Camp was full of secondhand items. The previous owners left many books. I devoured all (and I do mean all) of the short stories in the hard-bound series of Readers' Digest stories from the '70s and any other beach books on the shelf. Aside from the presence of these books, I found little evidence that the previous owners spent much time at camp. The windows were painted shut and the deck was a practically a death trap. It slouched under our steps and its wood edges crumbled at our touch. Dad rebuilt it first thing.

Mom says that when she walked in for the first time after the mortgage closing with her cleaning bucket in hand, she was overwhelmed with the work to be done. Her best friend, who had come to help, gave her a shove to get started. I would have needed more than just a shove. Cobwebs, dirty windows, dead ants and mouse droppings surrounded her. A sticky sugar bowl sat in the center of the table. Once she got started, the grime gave way to warmth and Mom's special homey-ness.

As with all camps, our old stuff made its way there. We had threadbare sheets, hand-me-down dressers, an old wheat-field couch decorated with a mix of orange, brown, and tan flowers. Only half of the oven worked. It was enormous, glossy white with chrome trim, but so old its next home was the GE museum in downtown Schenectady. All in all, to have a camp was a great luxury. Mom's signature rack of personalized coffee mugs hung on the wall to the left telling the story of our family: *#1 cheerleader, #1 mom, S-G field hockey, Electricians light up your life...*

Large barn-style doors opened to a dirt floor basement that spanned the entire area of the house. The washer and dryer were in the basement. So were the skunks, chipmunks, and bats.

One day, while doing laundry with her 1930s ringer washer, Mom was ambushed by an enraged and potentially rabid chipmunk. Startled by the insane chipmunk and her own screams, Mom's hand, which was guiding one of Dad's flannel shirts into the ringer, crunched into the mechanism. In her panic, she threw the ringer in reverse and ran her hand back out. Later, she laughed about reversing the ringer rather than using the safety to pop it open. In fact, why didn't the safety pop open on its own? It was always popping open for jeans!

This minor accident was prompted by the skunk family living in our basement. Even though Dad went to the Humane Society to get Havahart traps to catch skunks, driving a mile or two away to release them in the wilderness, they found their way back. In those days, before there was a bat crisis, bats were plentiful around camp and a few made their way into the basement, hanging from the rafters in the quiet damp back where the dirt floor sloped up to meet the floor of the house in an ever-closing gap which followed the contour of the hill the house was built on. I can picture Mom doing laundry cautiously trying to look like an appliance.

At the end of that particular day, she sat on the cocktail dock entertaining everyone with her Claudia vs. wildlife story. Later that summer our neighbor painted a sign that said *Wild Life Preserve* and presented it to Mom with a grand flourish as a forever memory.

I would like to think that after that eventful day, I would not even *need* to be asked to run up the hill and get her a beer and Kleenex. Let's face it, she risked life and limb (somewhat literally) to provide us with clean clothes. But that's the mom in me talking. I am sure I didn't give a crap. I was a teenager!

We never truly appreciate our mothers until we grow up.

Kim Perone

Wall of Fame

You are never too old to have your mother put your drawing on the fridge. Recently, my nephew Owen was visiting. Mom purchased a roll of brown paper and we spread it out and taped it to the floor, dumping a 24-pack of crayons on top. My two-year-old nephew tossed me a "geen" crayon and said, "Here you go, Aunt Kimmy." Wow, a full sentence! My sister would be proud.

We all colored. Owen drew swirls of interconnected Os. Mom made flowers. I drew our dog Comet. I knew that Owen would be able to recognize the picture right away. I didn't have any grand plans to make it look realistic, but the short, shaggy, white dog with a black nose was better than I expected. I sat back admiring my own work. "Well, how 'bout that!" I thought. Behind Comet, I drew Owen's black lab, Marley. Owen said, "Commie... Barley!"

Mom said, "Hey, that's not bad!" and promptly whipped out her camera and took a picture of it. A few minutes later, Owen tore it up. The next day she sent me this email.

To Kimberly Perone
From: Mom
Sent: Mon 3:05 PM

Kim,
I do have a record of your crayon drawing. As soon as I download the picts from my camera I'll

send to you. You did a real good job. Worthy of being on the refrigerator.

Love,
Mom

She is *good.*

We are both filled with such joy after a visit with Owen, who calls himself 'Owney.' Since my sister is gone, we are his stand-in mothers. We will always be Nanny and Auntie, but we are as close as it gets to his mother genetically. We talk like her, think something like her, and most importantly, love him as much as she would.

Mom and I will do our best to ensure that he feels the love of his mother through us. My brother-in-law is an extremely loving man and he and Owen make a good, solid team. I know there are many days when Owen is Omar's reason for getting up in the morning and also many days when he curses God for leaving him with all of this responsibility and taking his beautiful wife.

Next week when we visit them in Connecticut, Mom and I will get to pick Owen up at daycare and meet his teachers. Whenever we are with Owen we take millions of photos. I upload them to the sharing website like my sister did. We hug and kiss him too much, if that is possible, which I don't think it is. We took him to sit on Santa's lap at Christmas; we took him to JC Penney's for formal photos. All things that Mom did with us.

When my sister and I were growing up, my mother filled the wall across from our couch with framed photos. The center, an 11" x 16" framed picture from Olan Mills of my sister and me in matching outfits, stared down from its proud post. The beige satin blouses with gathering around the wrists and neckline and the brown velour skirts were made by Mom. Perfect holiday out-fits. I was eight and Kristen was three. It was a profile shot so my buckteeth had nowhere to hide. I never really liked the photo, as it reflected an awkward stage for me. The justification of my need for braces was never more evident. Kristen, on the other hand, looked incredibly cute and very much like Owen looks now.

Around this center masterpiece was a display like I had never seen in any other house. There were a hundred framed photos stretching from the front door through the dining room. We lived in a bungalow, so from the moment you walked in the front door you were greeted by our wall of fame spanning all the way to the kitch-en in the back of the house. There were all the typical formal shots, some with just Kristen and me and others with Mom and Dad, too. There was a picture of me as a baby with a stuffed lion. The picture was colored in with what looked like pencil the way they used to before colored pictures were the norm. There was a picture of Kris-ten in her christening gown. Mom and I appear in pictures with our long hair and middle parts, Kristen with barrettes and a big smile, and Dad with his trademark dark brown woolly bear hair, beard, and mustache combo.

This wall of fame, or shame (think protruding teeth), was a conversation starter. Visitors to our house always commented on it. It was seen by my friends, boyfriends, and other relatives. Rather than embarrassing us, it provided us with a sense of pride. It stared out at us in our daily lives, bolstering our self-esteem. It told our visitors that we were cherished by our parents. We felt loved.

When I asked my mother what made her put up so many photos, she said she was simply trying to cover the outdated wall paneling. So, it wasn't an activity prompted by an article in *Good Housekeeping* or *Parents* magazines after all. But for the record, she still gets credit. She took us to get our photos taken, she filled out the school picture forms, and she lovingly framed and hung these photos one by one, above the dry sink, above the television, next to the dining room table.

Mothers love their children. A mother's biggest fear is that something will happen to her child. Her next biggest fear is that something will happen to *her* and she will not be able to raise her child. The former, because it is a mother's greatest failure, regardless of fault; the latter, because no one will love your child as much as you do. I am speaking in general terms here, fully aware that there are some parents who abandon their children and others who adopt children and their love makes them their own.

I hope that my brother-in-law remarries a loving woman with room in her heart for her husband's offspring. *All of her husband's offspring.*

That day, when I was at Mom's playing with Owen, I saw that she had shoeboxes of photos sitting out and was beginning to put some in photo albums. These were old, yet not-so-old, photos. Me and my sister when we were each in college, both of our first apartments after college, Mom and Grammy at Easter, photos of baby Jack in my arms, little Stevie getting his haircut. Seeing these photos, I was hit with that familiar sense of pride, knowing that these are the most precious things Mom has besides our real selves.

Growing Up Together

My mother recalls telling her father she was pregnant. She was seventeen and just about to start her senior year in high school. How could you forget that? After he listened to her confession, he asked her, "Is that what you want to do?" meaning do you want to have the baby.

"Of course!" she replied, indignant that he even asked. Today, when she looks back she appreciates the fact that he was the only one of their parents thinking of her. What did *she* want to do?

The rest rushed Mom and Dad off to the Justice of the Peace— or so I thought. No, it was a surrogate court judge in another town. By going to a neighboring town and a surrogate judge, the notice wouldn't be in our town's paper. As if my grandparents' friends would just think they got married when they were thirteen or something and finally decided to have a family at eighteen!

Both Mom and Dad needed their parents to sign for the marriage since they were under twenty-one. While it seemed insensitive to rush these two kids off to a surrogate judge for marriage, it *was* 1968. I am sure at the time it was exactly the right way to help. Mom says, "I found out about all the other relatives who were in that same predicament." Many women get pregnant prior to marriage. Oh, you thought you were *premature,* did you?

After the brief marriage ceremony and parental signing, my grandparents brought my mother home and my father went to work. It was a Thursday afternoon in October. I picture her sitting on the couch in a pretty skirt pinching her growing waist and twiddling her thumbs looking around and thinking, *What do I do now?* (No doubt, she started cleaning.)

In February, Mom turned eighteen, Dad turned nineteen. I was born in March. Mom had an easy pregnancy, but tough labor. After many long and arduous hours, I was born—7 pounds, 2 ounces. Kimberly Ann. Poof, family! In photos, my parents look like kids. They *were* kids.

With little instruction, they became great parents. They followed their instincts and it worked. Whenever I hear of a teenager who is pregnant, I always say, "Hey, look how I turned out!" I don't promote or condone it, but the alternatives could be a mistake. I reinforce that although it might not be optimal, and yes, there are sacrifices to be made, it can work out very well.

My mother looked at me in the ensuing years and tried to imagine her life without me. She had options. The option my grandfather was referring to was adoption. She could leave school under the guise of *mononucleosis* or *going to another school,* give birth, come back to finish her senior year, and continue onto college and have a great life.

In 1968 abortion was illegal, but I am sure there were ways to find places to accommodate. It is controversial, but I like to separate the concept from any religious or personal opinions and think more about how it changes history. What if the child not born was supposed to do something significant in the world? What if that child was the scientist who would cure cancer? It is all philosophical. I don't judge. I just wonder.

Instead of all these other choices, my parents married and started a family. I naturally loved them both and still adore them today. Mom was encouraged by a friend to finish high school and get her degree. She only needed twelfth-grade English to get her diploma. She took the class while the friend babysat me, and she received her diploma.

More than once my mother told that me I actually kept my parents—those crazy kids—out of trouble. At first they were still hanging around with their friends, just bringing me with them. But when I was a toddler, I found a pill in the couch at one of these parties and handed it to my mother. Whether it was speed or LSD, we'll never know, but it scared Mom and they both realized the time had come for them to decline party invitations. The drug scene in 1970 was pretty vibrant and I am glad they had an additional reason to stay away from it.

Trouble, up to that point, had been my mother's middle name. A defiant Catholic school girl, she went to church daily but raided the envelope donation to buy candy at the corner store.

"You did??" I said incredulously.

"Yeah" she said, "and I also wanted to be a nun." As a kid, she never gave the hypocrisy a second thought. She wanted to be a nun, but then added, "We all did. Catholic school girls wanted to be nuns and the boys wanted to be priests. And later the same day, I was smoking behind the school." After some thought she added, "I started smoking when I was eleven and quit when I was eighteen. If everyone did it that way, they'd be a lot healthier."

Born in Schenectady and raised in a little house on Edgewood Avenue, Mom remembers the day in 1956 when a large trailer pulled up in front of the house. She was five years old. Looking out the window, her father beamed and said, "That's our new house!" She was devastated.

For the next six years they moved every year. Her father was a mobile home manager and they moved from Schenectady to Long Island, to New Jersey, then to Highland Falls (near West Point). Each time they moved in January, rather than at the beginning of the school year. Mom was always the new kid paraded in front of the class. *Everyone, this is Claudia. Say, hello Claudia. (Claudia, Daudia)*

When Mom was in middle school, her mother (my Grammy) decided she was leaving my grandfather because of his affair with a lady in the trailer park. (To be fair, that lady became his wife for thirty years until her death after suffering with Alzheimer's.) It must not have been easy to pick up and leave your husband in 1962. She went back upstate New York to live in the flat above her sister in their two-family house. My mother remembers having lawn furniture in the living room in the beginning. Grammy told me that when she was trying to get a job, the interviewers would ask her how she was going to work and take care of her daughters. She said accurately they were old enough to take care of themselves after school. "But what if they are sick?" she was asked. She did get the job. Grammy was not known for being a bold person, but I do believe her determination to make it on her own must have showed through enough to convince this company interviewer. This type of questioning is illegal today, thankfully.

I think this was about the time my mother's love of cleaning first kicked in. She helped my grandmother with household chores. Recently, she told me that they had mismatched sheets and even back then it bothered her if the fitted sheet and the top sheet didn't match. Today, she can't even sleep on wrinkled sheets!

After years of honing her cleaning and cooking skills to assist my working single grandmother, Mom was ready for wifedom. Or so she thought. Tuna casserole was the first meal my mother made as a new housewife. My father wanted to know where the meat was. Growing up, Mom rarely had meat. She certainly thought tuna qualified as meat. Grammy needed to stretch the dollar until it begged for mercy, naturally.

Parenthood suited my parents. I have many fond memories. Mom always says that you are as old as your kids are—meaning that if you have kids later in life they keep you young, but if you have them early you may feel older than you are but you will have freedom while you can still enjoy it. And, you are young enough to play—*really play*—with your grandchildren.

Although they were young, Mom and Dad made conscious choices about how our family would run. So while we were growing up, so were they.

Like many who marry young, they found that things can get sticky and tricky when the kids are grown. How do you want to spend the rest of your life? Theoretically, they were looking at forty more years.

Kim Perone

The Divorce

The year was 1992 and I was happily planning my wedding. Actually, I was happily getting married. As for the planning part, my best friend had to prod me at every task. *Did you get invitations? When are you going dress shopping? What did the caterer say?* Ugh. I didn't like the details. And I dreaded the dress. Honestly, I wear dark colors to look slimmer and now I was supposed to go and get a big puffy white gown on the day I am supposed to look my best?

Mom was so excited. She wanted us to pick the most expensive wedding location on our list. My parents were paying for the reception. You could say it was *our* wedding, Mom's and mine. No town court judge on a Thursday afternoon this time around. No siree, this wedding was going to be happy, white, and elegant, not to mention publicized. My future husband, Dave, did not like being told what to do being the fiercely independent type, so he was wary about my parents paying for the reception. It took some explaining that paying for their daughter's wedding was important to my parents and that it is just plain silly to complain about parents trying to do something nice for you. He started to soften.

During the planning process, Mom took me out to dinner at Ferrari's, the Italian restaurant down the street from my house. Dave and I were living together at the time in an old neighborhood in Schenectady, which was originally settled by Polish and Italian immigrants and interestingly (or commonly), both of our families at one point or another started out in the neighborhood.

I remember what Mom was wearing—a fashionable red dress with teeny, tiny blue flowers all over it. We ordered our drinks, and as the waitress walked away, Mom said very seriously, "I have something to tell you."

I replied in a way that had, oddly, become a mantra in my family, "Well I know you and Dad aren't getting divorced because how would you divide the camp?" (nervous chuckle) I didn't think I would hear what I was going to hear.

"We are seeing a marriage counselor."

Whoa...Hold...the...phone. I scrunched down over the table leaning toward her in that way people do when they reply to shocking information and whispered frantically, "What is going on?"

I wish I could recall what she said. The conversation is a blur of "Dr. Lloyd...financial control..." and "already gone." *Gone, gone, gone* echoed in my ears. Or was I the one who thought the word 'gone'? I sensed it was over. Later, in conversations with my father, he said Mom was not interested in the marriage counselor. She had already made up her mind.

My parents divorced. Mom had a life to lead. She was exactly the age I am now, forty-one. It was hard for everyone, including Mom. She deserved some charge over her own life and to get it she walked away from friends, the camp, and left her family unhappy to lose a beloved in-law. My sister and I demonized her. I wish I'd understood sooner. It wasn't about how it affected *our* lives.

My sister, while stressed about the situation, made out like a bandit. Don't get me wrong, when she came home from college and had to choose who to stay with and had to go back and forth, it

Kim Perone

was not fun. But she was a college student who could do anything she wanted. "Travel throughout Europe after graduating? Sure, that's wonderful!"

What? Are these my parents? They would not have let me do that; it is fair to say they would have forbidden it. I was twenty-one, and I would have listened, believing their authority over me. They would say, "Oh, no, you are not travelling through Europe, get real! You are paying back these college bills, pronto!"

Kristen became a vegetarian. "Vegetarian? Sure, we'll never eat meat again as a family," was the response.

I once regaled Kristen's friend and her mom, along with my mom, with a rendition of what my mother's response would be to me turning vegan. "Guess what we are having for dinner, Kim. Meatloaf! WhaaaaaHahahahahahah!"

My mother laughed as heartily as meat, knowing it would have been true. During the ensuing years, everywhere we went, Mom's house, Dad's house, we ate vegetable lasagna. Dave said, "If we have to eat one more veggie lasagna, I am going to go crazy!"

But I must admit, I didn't want to travel through Europe or give up meat. Their accommodation of Kristen's plans made sense. They were now under pressure and in competition, rather than the unbreakable wall of discipline of their former married parental selves.

Several years before their separation, after years as a stay-at-home mother, Mom added a part-time job at the local department store, then another at the 'figure salon,' the precursor to women-only fitness clubs. The extra income was used to buy us special girl stuff. In particular, a mauve Gunne Sax dress with crocheted trim and matching crocheted high-heeled sandals for my eighth-grade dance. When I was sixteen, Mom started working full-time in the tax department of the State of New York. She started at the lowest level. She has since climbed several steps in position and many thousands of dollars in salary. So from that time until seven years later, she was happily working while I was graduating from high school and going to college, eventually making wedding plans.

As an optimist, and an adult child of divorce, I am happy to see both of my parents realize their dreams. My step-parents are extremely well suited to my parents' personalities and I love them. During the breakup, I just wanted peace and happiness for both of my parents.

I am confident they have found it.

Pearls of Wisdom

In my family, the pearls of wisdom my mother gave us were real pearls. It was Christmas a few years ago and she had saved her money and bought both of us girls Mikimoto pearl earrings, pearl necklaces, and bracelets. Her Miki-motto: every woman should have pearls and not need a man to give them to her.

My husband came unhinged. He did not say anything at the holiday event, but later voiced his opinion that it was an assault on his credibility, that she was insinuating that he would not ever buy me pearls or jewelry. I assured him this was not the case. I remember accompanying my dad to the jewelry store for birthdays and other holidays. It was not a sentiment about men directly, but rather on the independence of women.

After years as a young housewife in the '70s, and investing in family in the '80s, in the '90s she had finally found personal and financial freedom.

Mom knows well that Dave has always supported my independence, never imposing money rules or restrictions on me. I try not to abuse this respect. Neither of us is an extreme spender or extreme saver. If you asked him, he would say I like shopping too much, but I also work very hard and can buy what I want. I do not have expensive tastes, nor does Dave. In the early years of our marriage, when I was a full-time student, and now, as a full-time writer, I exercise caution and restraint. I know my weaknesses and try to avoid the siren song of shoe- or bookstores.

Mom's background, a teenage bride and housewife for many years, led to an extreme enjoyment in buying small luxuries. Both of my parents worked very hard and sacrificed, because I came along so early. Dad went to school full-time and worked full-time. Mom took care of me at home in their new mobile home.

It was only in my late teens that I learned that my father had been accepted to Northeastern University in Massachusetts. Rushing off to the judge in October and the hospital delivery room in March changed those plans. Dad is extremely bright and has always cheered our educational and career accomplishments, despite the sidelining of his.

Dad adored my sister and me and never seemed to think of what might have been. He worked hard as an electrician, was a member of the union board, and a teacher of apprentices. My parents became successful members of the middle class. The camp, while a financial stretch for them at the time, was Dad's paradise. My father would look out on the lake with his arm around my mother and say, "I wonder what the poor people are doing right now."

They made many sacrifices and grew up together. Their separation really only marked the beginning of *rest* of their lives. After the dust settled, it was clear that they had completely different personalities and the future held a change that would enhance all of our lives in many ways.

My father met Rena. She is gorgeous, quiet, and loving, enjoys nature and animals, and loves us all: grown-up daughters, sons-in-law, and grandchildren. She could live barefoot in the woods. Staying outside until bedtime during the beautiful northeast summers, her long dark hair and long lean legs making her look like

Kim Perone

Pocahontas, she has nurtured flowers, domesticated chipmunks, and birds practically land on her hand.

Mom loves her job and works long hours and enjoys expensive things bought with her own hard-earned money. She has traveled the country and the world, she has experienced as much as she can of fine dining, fine jewelry, and the fine arts. Most recently she has renovated her entire townhouse. She vows never again to share a checkbook or a mortgage. My mother's significant other (SO) Dan, who is also a common-law husband at this point, respects her independence, which would make many a man shudder with fear.

Dan also embraced our family and is a beloved member. He is quite independent himself and will honestly tell her whether or not he wants to join her travels, based on his interest in the trip or interest in enjoying alone time at home. Mom approaches sightseeing the way she vacuums. And sometimes, Dan appreciates, not hearing the vacuuming while he is watching television. Mom is fine whether he wants to join her or not.

After her life changed from frustrated housewife to self-sufficient working woman, Mom abruptly packed away all the tools of her former life of arts and crafts and became the sophisticated lady of the world, with only a few moments of fame in the midst of travel. A few notably famous projects include making teddy bears out of the yellow blankie that I wouldn't release until I was five, and creating a magnificent wedding cake for my sister's big day. She could bump both Martha Stewart and Rachel Ray off the airwaves if she wished.

My parents and my step-parents are exceptional people. While I joke about my 'pearls of wisdom,' they are just a symbol of everything I have gained from all of them. I thank them for giving me such a strong foundation and sense of humor, so that I am able to handle the challenges of life. All four of them have been there for me during the lightest and darkest of times of my adult life.

The Claudinator

"You have to work to have friends," says Mom. You have to work for many reasons, of course, but Mom says that work is all worth it for the friends you make. As if the time you spend with them is also part of the paycheck, she doesn't take friendship for granted.

It is true that much of life is experienced with work friends. You spend so much time at work. The extra appreciation of work friendship is warranted since my mother lost all her previous friends in my parents' divorce. We were friends with the family next door at camp. They all belong to Dad now. He lives there. Mom and Dad were best friends with my father's friend from high school and his wife.

My best friend from high school, Brenda, works in a different unit, but the same place as Mom. They both work for the State of New York's Taxation and Finance Department. "Job security," Mom says, "*we* bring in the money."

Mom is probably the only state worker in the western world who works late. She loves her job. She wants to learn everything she can. She started as a grade 3 in 1986, the bottom level, and is now a 23. Brenda has known my mother for the twenty-six years we have been friends. She doesn't like to hug my mother because, she says, "Your mom's head is armpit level!"

Mom is tiny. When looking at photographs, I often see people do a 'double-take.' They can't figure out what is wrong with the picture, but then I point out that I look huge because my mother is 4'11". They all reply the same way, "Ohhhhh, that's it." Because people generally think of me as small at 5'2 ", the pictures look odd because I look at least 5'8" inches in photos standing next to Mom. Mom is miniature. She is the size of an eleven-year-old boy.

"At work, people know Claudia is coming around the corner at work because she has this fast 'clickclickclickclick' sound when she walks," Brenda says. "We call her the Claudinator."

Mom moves fast, thinks fast, and has no time to waste. She has traveled to Europe—Scotland, Ireland, Italy, and many places in the United States including Hawaii, California, and Nevada.

She likes to call us from all of her destinations. "I am at the top of the Hoover Dam, can you hear me?"

Stevie was only about eight when she was in Las Vegas. I said, "Talk to Nanny, she's in Las Vegas."

He said hello, then ran off hollering to Dave, "Hey Dad, Nanny's in Lost Vegas!"

"That sounds about right," Dave said.

Mom has even enjoyed the bad times at work. "I worked for a real wacko once," Mom says. Everyone knows that the state can only fire a worker if they assault another person, steal several thousand computers, or sell people's social security numbers. "But that is how I learned to handle difficult people. You need to outsmart them at their own game." Outsmart and outlast, that is her motto.

Back when I was pregnant the first time, I mentioned I was considering staying home after the baby was born. She was terribly concerned. We fought on the phone. I was only twenty-five and couldn't really appreciate my mother's experience as a stay-at-home mom with little control or independence. I ended up working full-time, but only three days per week and it all worked out fine. In fact, it was the best of both worlds. But Mom is adamant that work for a woman ensures she has control. She is fond of noting that Dan is just a renter. He steps out of line, he's evicted.

Dave says, "She has *a lot* of baggage." And it is true.

Larry says, "She's an emotional hoarder."

Oh, you haven't met Larry yet. Let me introduce my brother Larry.

Kim Perone

My Brother Larry

My mother's friend Larry is the kind of friend that sitcoms are built around. Raising his eyebrows and shrugging with a funny comment on something she just did, he is the "Chandler" of Friends for my mother. He is simultaneously a foundation, institution, and comic relief for my mother.

They met at work and I call him "my brother Larry," because at my grandmother's (Mom's mother) funeral, Grammy's friend Virginia thought Larry was my mother's son. Virginia's eyesight was seriously suspect. I hope she didn't drive there.

Larry doesn't look younger than my mother. He is in his late fifties, like Mom. They make quite a pair. He is as large as she is small; she is as short as he is tall. Mom dyes her hair and Larry doesn't have any. Now that I think about it, Larry and my mother are soul twins. They have been perfectly platonic friends for nearly twenty years. He spends all his time making fun of my mother in a way that no one else ever could. She gives him so much material. *And they laugh and laugh.*

At the funeral, in 1995, Mom sent Larry and Brenda to her townhouse to get things ready before people arrived from the funeral home, knowing we wouldn't be able to scoot out early.

"Your mom gave Larry a list of everything we were to set out on the table and everything we were to do, and on the bottom it said *'and do anything Brenda tells you to do,'*" Brenda recounts.

"Ketchup was on the list, but I thought maybe that was just thrown in there because of the sandwich condiments. So I questioned whether it really needed to come out. Why?" she shrugged her shoulders. "I mentioned this to Larry and he looked concerned. He was obviously torn between the list and what I was saying.

"Eventually I said just to leave the ketchup in the fridge, I didn't think anyone needed it for sandwiches. When your mother arrived she looked at the table and said curtly, 'Where's the ketchup?' Larry pointed to me and said, 'It's all her fault.'"

No doubt he was terrified of my mother's wrath for imperfection.

Since the mid-'90s were the early years of my parents' divorce, you would think that if Mom had a male friend, it would be a boyfriend, but she was more interested in her freedom than anything else. Larry was a very safe companion. Each year Larry, Mom, and their friend Gail went to the ballet in Saratoga. Gail and Mom were all dolled up and Larry made a good escort.

"Larry has the only wife who would drop her husband off to go to the ballet with his two girlfriends!" Mom joked. He is everyone's friend, everyone's rock, and an entertainer with humor as dry as the Sahara Dessert. I am glad my mother has a friend like Larry and I like thinking of him as a brother. He's my brother Larry.

Larry told me about their trip to the Yankee games many years ago. "She orders a beer as big as her. I say, 'Claudia, you don't even know what's going on do you?' and she says, 'I don't care.'"

Mom, the independent woman on her own, bought the townhome after a short stint in an apartment. She was a working woman, with grown children, travel plans, a fur coat, new expenses, and maybe, just maybe, a shopping problem a bit beyond her. But she was managing fine in general.

In the winter of 1994 and she came down with the flu, "the real flu" as she puts it, and because she was so incredibly sick, she started having anxiety attacks and hallucinating She made Larry watch Steve Martin movies while discussing every person they knew who had financial troubles. Larry was the only person invited into the realm of vulnerability.

"At the time I was $4,000 in debt and thought I needed help with managing my money. Can you imagine such a crazy thing? $4,000 is nothing, I was soon to learn!" Mom says.

The '90s was also the time of the great dotcom boom. Mom took her half of the family assets and invested heavily in the market. At the time, Dave and I were newly married and she was trying to get us to buy investments online. This was a bit advanced for us. We wanted to work through a real person who was responsible for our money. The kind of advisor we could sit down with annually and review our investments. Giving our money over to some faceless individual in virtual space in 1994 seemed Crazy, with a capital C. But here was Mom with her Yahoo! stock soaring. She was actually shouting 'yahoo.'

"It is *so* easy," she said.

Larry was her computer wizard, so she was all hooked up online and feeling confident long before Al Gore took credit for the internet. We were just beginning our cyber-journey, but Larry, like a good brother, also came to our house and got us hooked up online for the first time.

When Mom was sick with the flu and worried about her overspending, I didn't realize that she was spending approximately $10,000 to $20,000 more per year than she earned, financed by her investment gains. She was siphoning off profits of her investments. However, in hindsight, that was money that would have evaporated anyway when the market corrected. The dotcom boom came back to reality with a pop and over-inflated stocks came down to reasonable prices. Only my mother could make a good investment out of overspending!

And this is the kind of thing that fascinates Larry about my mother. She is entertaining and makes good muse for his inner comedian.

Our funny, lovable brother has been battling Lou Gehrig's Disease, otherwise known as Amyotrophic Lateral Sclerosis (ALS), for the past two years. While it has slowed him down, it certainly hasn't dampened his humor. When we were talking the other day, he was telling me that the diagnosis of ALS is actually the elimination of other potential diseases. Doctors test for MS, Parkinson's, and a variety of other things. When they come up negative, what is left is ALS.

"You should have told them, 'Hey, don't rush on my account, go back to the drawing board and come back with another diagnosis,'" I said. He laughed.

"Or better yet, you need House." I add. The mention of our favorite television show, where the Vicodin-addicted doctor relentlessly puzzles over mystery diagnoses, brings a nod of recognition.

Larry tells me how my mother, forever the optimist, responded to the diagnosis. "She said, 'Well, it's good it started in your legs. You don't use your legs for anything much, but you like to use your head to talk and for the computer, right?'" All true. Sadly, ALS can attack your bottom half or top half first. Mom said she heard a guy golfed up until the end but couldn't speak or eat. Larry would definitely rather have his speech and Mom is right. He says all of this with a smile of his face, amused again. There is a soul fit.

Kristen's cancer diagnosis coincided in the fall of 2008 co-incided with the ALS walk Mom had joined in honor of Larry. She had all her donations in already, but we wanted to spend the weekend at Kristen's house in Connecticut rather than Albany. So she sent an email to her donors that she was walking in Fairfield instead. She had her team tee-shirt and not surprisingly, made Kristen, baby Owen, and me tee-shirts to match. They were bright royal blue with white letters across the front that announced the team name "Brooks Brigade," to reflect Larry's last name. We wore long sleeved white shirts under them. Mom supplied them as well.

"We're all going to walk for Larry," Mom said. We did conduct our part of the walk around the town on that beautiful fall day, toting little four-month-old Owen with us. We took pictures to prove it. They were sent with the thank yous to donors.

Later that day, Mom and I walked to the drug store to pick up some vitamins and herbal remedies, while Kristen was putting Owen down for a nap. Mom had a list, from an Internet search of course, of a number of items that were supposed to help with cancer.

While we were perusing the shelves, an old man asked my mother where the diabetes supplies were. She promptly directed him to the next aisle where she thought the items might be. It took me a minute, but I got it. When I did, I waited for Mom to get it. I didn't say anything, I just waited.

In my head I counted 1, 2, 3 and, as if on cue, she looked at me and said, "I guess that guy thought I worked here."

"You know why?" I asked.

"No. Why?"

I pointed to her shirt. Brooks Brigade. The two of us were

standing in Brook's drug store, with matching uniforms. And of course, she looked like she owned the place. We laughed.

"Larry's going to love that story," I said.

Remote Options

"I don't know what she did, but she broke Dan…It's really sad to see. I put in a missing person report—he's there in body, but not there," Larry tells me.

Mom laughs and says, "I did break him. At least I use my powers for good, not evil!"

I ask them to tell me the famous remote story.

"We were at an after-work function and Larry was my designated driver. We stopped at the Krispy Kreme so I could pick up doughnuts on the way home. It was about 7:30 PM," Mom starts. "Dan had just gotten his monster TV and I wanted Larry to see it. But as we were clicking the buttons on the remote to get it turned on, we accidentally knocked it off cable, but we didn't know what we did, just that it was screwed up."

Dan was not really an angry person at the time, just someone who grew up in that family dynamic where it is common to think everyone is making you crazy. His new television was 52" wide, just the right size for a Jets fan. It towered over the room. Dan has two favorite hobbies, golfing and watching television. He did, at that time, have a very stern demeanor which is unexpected for someone in a relationship with Mom. But she loved that she had total freedom to come and go as she pleased, so his gruffness was a minor irritation. And of course for humor, she had Larry.

"Just then we hear the garage door open. It's Dan coming

home. Just as Dan's walking in from the kitchen, Larry throws the remote up in the air and it lands right in my hand. Dan looks at me and says to Larry, looking at the TV, 'What did she do to screw up the TV?'"

"I really thought he was going to kill her," Larry says. "I checked the paper the next day."

Dan was furious. "He looked like Jack Nicholson in *The Shining*," Larry says making a happy, yet crazy face.

"I am drunk, but I am calling the cable company," Mom says. "I say to Dan, 'Give me the goddam remote!' which he grabbed from me earlier, and he does."

The cable company tells her to go behind the television and check the cables. While she is doing this, Dan is yelling "Don't go back there!" I can imagine he thinks his world is spinning out of control. He is pissed that Mom is drunk this early in the evening, no doubt (I know how that feels) and he is now remarkably upset that his brand new television is projecting a blank screen. *Utter helplessness... A world...gone mad.*

"Larry just, like, bolted. I wanted to yell out the door *'Chicken! Chick-en!"* Mom adds.

Larry astutely saw this as his opportunity to sneak out and avoid more of this common-law marital dispute. "I didn't want to be there when he killed her," Larry says defending himself.

"Dan just sat there on the couch with his arms crossed looking like Joe Torre," Mom says. Dan does indeed look like the former Yankees manager Joe Torre right down to the I-look-mad-when-I-am-just-neutral look of his face, and thick head of hair.

Mom gets the television back on and working. Dan says, "How did you screw this up?"

"You are such an ass," she replies. "I fixed it. Larry screwed it up! Not me!"

She said she could see the wheels turning in his head, thinking that if Larry could screw it up, he, a fellow male, could, too. Fear shadowed his face.

Mom starts giggling.

"What are you snickering at?" Dan asks, still clearly pissed off.

"You! I am laughing at you!" she says.

She storms upstairs and gets into the shower. "Don't tell Dan, but I was bumping into the sides of the wall in the shower because I was so drunk, and laughing and laughing."

Later that night when they climbed into bed, she's still giggling.

"What is wrong with you?!" he asks.

"I laughed for days. The way the remote fell perfectly in my hand. I still laugh when I think about it. I wish I could bottle that laughter and sell it," Mom says.

Since those early years of their relationship, Dan has really softened up. That's what Larry means when he says she broke him.

"I used to say to Dan, 'Let's get her going' and now he says, 'Don't get me in trouble.'"

At my niece Cheryl's wedding, Mom and Dan, my sister Kris and her husband Omar, and Brenda and her husband Paul all sat at our table. Dave and Steve were in the wedding. Our friends Brenda and Paul are consummate 'ballbusters.' One year they even had that pre-printed on their Christmas cards. *"Merry Christmas, Love, The Ballbusters."*

We were all sitting together talking, reminiscing about the old disco days, and it emerged that Dan liked Donna Summer. Brenda's father was a huge Donna Summer fan, too. So Paul, being Paul, went to the DJ and requested Donna Summer's "The Last Dance" for Dan. When the DJ called it out, Paul pushed Dan to the dance floor. He grabbed my mother and they disco-danced like their lives depended on it.

Dan knew all the moves, but he was throwing my mother around like a rag doll. Her tiny little figure was flying around the dance floor. She was smiling like a pro and doing her best to make it all look smooth. He was not happy being forced out into the middle of the dance floor to solo disco dance due to a practical joke.

That night they got into the biggest fight of their relationship.

"What is wrong with you?!" she just couldn't take angry-Dan anymore. She was done.

"False advertising, that's what it is," she told me when we were alone. "When we met he liked to dance and drink wine. Now, nothing!" That is the complaint of many and she acted surprised.

Mom says she wanted to send Paul a thank you card. I am sure Dan didn't. I made sure we never mentioned Donna Summer in Dan's presence again.

They were at the breaking point and Mom was done. That was the "last dance" for Mom. This must have shaken Dan and he needed to reexamine his anger, like most men do at some point in their life. Mom couldn't be around it anymore.

Luckily he didn't want to end their relationship and he stood his ground. He let some of his man-anger go after that. Larry's

right. She *did* break him, like a wild horse. He's now domesticated.

Fountain of Youth

It was a big weekend, a moment of truth. Our mother and my sister's soon-to-be mother-in-law would meet for the first time. Mrs. M, as described by Kristen, was a very proper and stern woman who, Kristen felt, had not warmed up to her yet. Now that the engagement was official, there were signs of progress; perhaps her formal manner only made her *seem* less than friendly. Surely, we would make a good impression. After all, we are so friendly we can make up for any shortfall.

The idea was to create an activity for the meeting. What would be more perfect than a drive to Darien to visit the prospective site of the wedding? We climbed into my SUV, Kristen drove, Mrs. M sat in the seat of honor, and Mom and I were in the back with my son Steven between us. He was ten years old at the time and irked to be with us rather than with the guys who were bonding at the golf course. I stopped short of telling him that ten years prior I thought he was going to be a girl and how nice this little outing would have been then because he would have *wanted* to be with us.

My mother had braces on her teeth. At fifty-five, she was taking care of old business fixing teeth that had always bothered her. My son was just about to get his braces. Mrs. M remarked that fortunately neither of her children needed braces. My mother piped in, "Thank goodness for braces, because the kids really needed them."

"Yes," I added, "buck teeth with a space in front tend to run in the family." I shuddered. Thank you, Mom and Dad! I cannot even imagine being an adult with the teeth I had. It is one thing to have crooked teeth, but buck? Space in front? I looked like Spongebob Squarepants.

"Oh yes," my mother said, "Thank goodness Kristen had braces, her teeth were unbelievably bad!"

"Mom, my teeth were exactly the same," I chimed in.

"No, no," she said, "your sister's teeth were way worse."

At least I tried. I chuckled to myself, amazed that my mother is embarrassing my grown sister with her soon-to-be mother-in-law. Mrs. M was probably picturing her future grandchildren as we spoke—little SpongeBobs. She had high hopes for better dental genes, I am sure. Later, when we were laughing at the exchange, my mother noted that she meant to point out how beautiful Kristen is now. Kristen just shrugged her shoulders with mock confusion, like, "What the…? Help!"

As we drove through the neighborhood, the homes increased in size leading us to a beautifully landscaped estate with a circular drive in front of a looming white house with black shutters. No cookie-cutter hotel wedding here. It was classic and sophisticated, just like my sister. She had decided to have a minister marry them at the location, rather than get involved in selecting the right church. This probably was not Mrs. M's favorite idea, being an Irish Catholic from New York City, but Kristen and Omar were in their thirties and paying for the wedding themselves. It was clearly their show. Plus Omar's father is a Lebanese immigrant of the Muslim faith. I imagine Mr. and Mrs. M grappled with their own faith decisions in the early years. Catholicism won, probably due to the proximity of the maternal grandmother. Mr. M celebrates the Muslim holidays, but has never felt the need to impose the rituals

Kim Perone

on the rest of the family. Neither his wife nor children minds eating in his presence during the fasting of Ramadan.

The benefit of interfaith marriage is the openness it creates in thoughts of God and heaven. Counter intuitively, it always reminds me that we are all one despite the differences.

We were unable to get inside the house in Darien; however, Kristen described the reception plans by pointing toward areas of house where there were large open rooms for cocktail areas, dressing rooms, photos sessions, and the dance floor. She noted that vows would take place outside in the area where we were standing. The chairs for guests would be aligned around a center sculpture fountain. The fountain, a cherub pouring water out of a bucket, looked more like he was peeing out of a bucket than pouring. It was autumn and the water was slimy and full of decaying leaves, but with the proper setup, this location would look quite lovely. Next year at this time, we would be enjoying a most elegant affair.

While we three women peeked in windows to see as much as we could from the outside, we heard a loud splash behind us. I whipped around in fear that my son had fallen in, but there he was, sheepishly standing on the side of the fountain. But the cherub was gone.

"What...did...you...do!?" I asked him in my nastiest mommy voice.

"I just put my foot on the edge of it," he said with a shrug.

My sister and I look around in a knee jerk reflex to check that no one saw us damaging the property. While we were getting ready to bolt—*Okay, tour's over, nothing to see her*—my mother looked at Steven and says "Get your socks and shoes off, we're going in!" He looked at her with eyes as big as dinner plates, while she began taking off her shoes and knee highs, rolled up her pants and jumped into the slimy cold water and began pulling the cherub up to put him back on the pedestal. Steve went in behind her, and at this point I had no choice but to jump in out of shame and obligation. We couldn't fix the hose that made the cherub pee, or pour water out of the bucket, but the wrong had been righted.

As Mom climbed out, Mrs. M pulled a hanky from her purse, waving it at my mother, "Claudia, use this to dry off your feet."

Kristen and I complimented our mother on her quick action. My sister laughed, noting she had her camera the whole time and yet didn't think to take any picture of the funny event for posterity. Mom gave us a silver-tooth smile.

As we walked out of the courtyard, convinced we had done enough damage for one day, we laughed again, making sure my son knew we were not laughing at him, but at the whole situation. We went out to lunch and continued bonding.

Did we make a good first impression? I am not sure, but it was hysterical and memorable. And in my family, funny memories are the ultimate achievement in life.

Kim Perone

Mother's Milk

I started drinking in my thirties. I spent my twenties as the bored sober one, drinking Diet Cokes and driving everyone home. In my teens, I had watched my parents party. They drank beer at summer parties until they fought. I was generally caught in the middle. Just like that cartoon where the boss kicks the husband, husband kicks the wife, wife kicks the kid, and kid kicks the dog. I was the kid. I never kicked the dog. In my teens, whenever they fought, I always ended up getting involved somehow. If I asked when dinner was, my mother felt that it was an attempt to oppress her by forcing the domestic role upon her. But it was not me she had an issue with. I was just wondering if I should make my little sister boxed macaroni and cheese.

All in all, conflict between my parents was mild—no crashing dishes or overturned furniture. I cannot imagine how hard that must be.

Basically, my parents would drink too much and became aggravated with each other. It altered their judgment and I was old enough to see what was going on, so when it came to alcohol, I would not relax my own control. That easy, falling release felt awful to me.

It worked out very well in the early years of my marriage. I was the designated driver everywhere we went. My husband is patterned more after my parents' generation—the end of the boomers—than mine, genXers; those for whom the drinking age was eighteen, meaning you could drink easily at fifteen. I however, had to wait until I was twenty-one. By then, I was addicted to Coca-Cola.

Mom and Dad were quiet fighters, loving parents, but woeful opposites. They were married young and they loved my sister and me and they did love each other, as I have described. They had tremendous chemistry. The moment Mom saw my father at Candyland, the local teen hangout in the '60s, she asked her friend, *"Who is he?"* They went to different high schools and her cousin, Linda, introduced them. I am surely a love child!

After the divorce, Mom traded in her beer and beer belly for Merlot and a tummy tuck. Dan likes New York City, Broadway shows, and fine dining. He likes to "peel the lettuce" as he calls it, referring to spending money in New York City. Mom says, "He had me at Merlot." She never knew guys could drink wine. Eventually we found out that Merlot is really the only wine he knows and he never drinks more than one glass with dinner out, which makes him a perfect designated driver.

Both my parents still drink. Not too much, but not too little either. Dad gets gout and Mom can't give up her two glasses of wine each night. However, when Kristen was about to give birth in the spring of 2008, Mom knew she should not drink wine every night because she might be called at any hour of the day or night to go to Connecticut for the birth. The moment of joy was coming!

She decided to switch from wine to milk. Once she did, she picked up a new habit. Mom said that she was enjoying milk each night, putting it in a wine goblet. It was even becoming—What did she say? —a desire. She was going through a gallon a week. I laughed. She literally switched jugs. She gave up her gallon of Ernest and Julio Gallo wine for a gallon of Moo Juice. If she was

Kim Perone

pulled over by the police they might ask where she was hiding the Oreos. "No officer, I really, no."

"Well, ma'am, you have a ...mustache." No more purple teeth just a milk mustache.

It was great to see her ability to transfer the addictions. I do think milk is the anti-wine. If I feel tipsy and want to top off before bed, I have a bowl of cereal or ice cream and it negates the wine. (This is important information!)

As it turns out, she did get the call, rushed off to Connecticut, and was completely sober for the three-hour drive and the momentous occasion of my nephew's birth. A boy! Another boy in our family—Owen "Got Milk" Mureebe was born in May 2008. He, too, likes milk.

Kim Perone

My Eggs Over Easy

Mom and I were in her car driving back from Connecticut. Her new mint green Pontiac Vibe, which could not match her personality any better, bucks and bumps so much that I feel like we are two inches from the pavement. Cars and couches must be carefully selected to suit their owners, and while the car drives like a U-haul trailer, it is small and can hold tons. Just like Mom.

As we drove, Mom says, "Oh, I forgot to tell you something."

"Oh no, what?" I say, full of dread and bracing myself for more bad news.

"I told your sister she could have your eggs, but I didn't get a chance to ask you first."

I feel the relief wash over me and my laughter bubble up in the place of fear. "But of course," I say. "She can have them!" Laughing and thinking, *I would turn them over easy.* "If she wants them, that is, but for full disclosure, I am turning forty in a few months so I am not sure I make a perfect egg donor. I guess some of the genes are right."

My mother says the funniest things as if they are completely serious and she did not intend them to be funny, but I suspect she intends the humor. That must be where I get my sense of humor. It is a Goldie Hawn ditzy blonde style. In fact, when it comes to ditzy blondes of the '70s my mother was 'every woman'. When I was growing up, she looked so much like Sally Struthers in *All in the Family* that people could not for the life of them keep her name straight. Everyone called her Gloria, rather than Claudia.

My husband Dave calls her Hurricane Claudia. She earned that title when she visited my sister in Louisiana at the time of a hurricane. It wasn't called Claudia, maybe it was Elaine or Doug, but it veered off and did not hit them. Dave says it's because there was already a hurricane in town!

My mother is a powerful force. She is a mini-framed, bleach-blonde ball of fire and whatever you do, don't get in her way. She has a list, she has people to see and places to go, and nothing can stand in her way. Not even destroyed eggs.

My eggs became relevant because as I mentioned previously my sister was diagnosed with cancer in the fall of 2008. Chemotherapy would destroy her eggs. She had just given birth to Owen, her first child, and the thought of going from giving birth to becoming barren was difficult news to swallow. She and my brother-in-law were just starting their family. But Hurricane Claudia was there to ensure clear minds prevailed and there was a focus on priority.

"Forget your eggs. You can have your sister's if you need them." *Next problem, please.*

Near Death Experience:
The Typhlitis

Kristen's appointment with a plastic surgeon regarding the removal of a lump in her leg, revealed her cancer. Several months prior, the small lump, located at the top of her right inner thigh, was examined by a doctor who said it was just fatty tissue. His advice was to have it removed if it began to bother her. Kristen was six months pregnant at the time, so she said it was no bother. Owen was born in May 2008 and we descended upon Connecticut in a flurry of estrogen and baby mania. Mom and I were in our glory with Kristen and her new baby and practically move in to help out. Unbeknownst to us, we would eventually do just that.

For the first chemo treatment in November 2008, we all looked at our schedules and came up with a 'helper' schedule which had Mom going to Connecticut during the week, taking Kris to her chemotherapy appointment and staying another day, and then Dad and I would come Friday for the weekend. Omar had a trip scheduled with his new employer to the company headquarters in Atlanta. Kristen had insisted that he still go, that it would be okay. We had it covered. She would feel sick and we would take care of her and Owen.

Omar had just accepted another job and notified his employer, also Kristen's employer, the week before Kristen was diagnosed.

After waiting several weeks to get in to see the plastic surgeon, the appointment turned out to be the beginning of a serious journey. The x-ray determined that this was far from a cosmetic situation. As she stood in my kitchen leaning against the counter in front of the sink on the Monday of Columbus Day weekend, she described the way the doctor immediately scheduled an MRI for her, in a slow and quiet voice. As I stared at her in rapt attention, she continued telling me the MRI revealed the lump, which was growing quickly now bothering her when she sat, was in fact a soft tissue tumor and they suspected it was a sarcoma. I could tell that their fast action and serious demeanor had put a fear in her and that she was about to embark on a serious path of treatment. The C word was used.

The test results confirmed it was cancer. A rare form of sarcoma, initially identified as rhabdomyosarcoma, which they eventually determined was Ewing's sarcoma. The doctors at her local hospital had some ideas on the course of action: removal and chemotherapy. Omar's sister Leila, a surgeon, promptly made important calls with all of the influence and the understanding of a medical professional that we needed. The result—Kristen would be treated at Memorial Sloan-Kettering in New York City by Dr. Brennan, the foremost expert in this type of sarcoma in the world. Thanks to Leila, we now had a slim ray of light in the darkness of the diagnosis. We thought if it is bad, at least we are in the center of the sarcoma universe.

Omar and Kristen went to the first chemotherapy appointment. The cancer killing had begun. Mom was there to babysit Owen and be there for Kristen, as she was destined to become ill. Two days later, I arrived to take over for Mom, and Dad arrived as backup for Omar. Owen was five months old.

The next morning, the pain in Kristen's bones had increased

significantly and Dad reminded me that Omar said we needed to check her temperature regularly. While I was tending to Kristen, the thermometer told us she had a fever. We called the oncologist. They took a message and in a few minutes I received a call from the doctor.

"Give her Tylenol for the pain and drive her to Norwalk Hospital's emergency room."

We made a quick decision that I would take her to the hospital and Dad would stay with Owen. I remember visiting her in the hospital when she had Owen, but couldn't remember exactly how to get there. We reclined the passenger seat and Kristen was lying in the fetal position focusing on her pain. I set my navigation unit to the hospital. When I took the first turn it fell on the floor and continued to guide me in a voice emanating from beneath my seat. She was clearly deteriorating. She was in so much pain, so quickly. She was in my passenger seat wracked with pain. In our haste, I had forgotten to give her Tylenol. Who would think that would make any difference?

At the hospital we abandoned the car and luckily there was a valet. I pulled her gently out and told her to lean on me while we walked in. They brought us directly to a room in the ER.

There wasn't a quick fix for her pain and fever. What transpired was an accelerating crisis. The staff's actions told me they were becoming more fearful for her health. After several hours in the ER, they told me that we were going to be moved to a room and she would be admitted to the hospital. After a long wait for a room to become available, we realized that the crisis had not passed. While they prepped her to move, I had some time in the lobby to call Omar. I explained the situation, feeling that I had failed him and Kristen on my watch.

In the hospital room, despite her pain and discomfort, they were going to take her blood pressure every 15 minutes for 24 hours, in each of three positions – lying down, sitting up, and standing. Every 15 minutes, all night long after all day in pain. I sat in the chair, trying to absorb her pain. If only I could.

Omar and my mother both came back to Connecticut and went directly to the hospital. I went back to the house to help my father with Owen, shower, and change. She was out of the woods. Dad needed to return home and go back to work. He was managing a large electrical project at a major employer in our area at the time. Mom came home to stay with me that evening and Omar stayed overnight at the hospital with Kris.

"When I think of how close we came to losing her..." Seeing my mother's shoulders slump and bounce with sobs, losing the rest of her unthinkable sentence, I was frozen. I was having some post-traumatic stress from the entire episode. I almost failed her. She left and things went horribly wrong.

Kristen suffered from typhlitis, which is an intestine infection that occurs in a very small percentage of chemotherapy patients. If the infection cannot be stopped, the doctors need to remove the infected part of the intestine, and they are limited to very small amount of removal or the patient will die.

Crisis averted. Luckily, after Kristen spent a full week in the hospital, she was back to normal. Kristen's near death experience had traumatized us all, but we were ready to get back to the real fight—the cancer. Mom began sending emails to her friends at work to keep all those loving and concerned people updated. After I received my copy of the email I asked Kristen, "Did you know Mom is describing your colon in exquisite detail to her colleagues?"

"I was trying to avoid thinking about it," she said and laughed.

Ahhhh, the power of the Internet.

Kim Perone

Off the List

The email updates were a good tool for my mother, who was missing more work due to trips to Connecticut. It also became a therapeutic tool. The pouring out of details about my sister's progress was an outlet, a pressure valve, on my mother's own concern. It was also a control mechanism, like vacuuming, that enabled Mom to take charge of the situation.

However, I worried that the therapy had too wide an audience for the depth of detail.

Update on Kristen

To: Team TI
From: Claudia
Date: Mon, 17 Nov 2008 10:16 a.m.

I know some of you are interested in Kris's progress so here is a quick update.

Kris is home and doing better now, but had a pretty rough time during the past two weeks. To make a long story short a common side-effect of the chemo drugs used to kill the cancer almost killed her. The specific side-effect, common with chemo treatment, was a low white blood cell count, the white blood cell called the neutrophil, to be specific. A low neutrophil count is one that is below 1500 per mm. Kris's was under 400, and considered 'severe'. Infections arise when the count is low, with the key sign of the infection being a fever. Kris had the fever, and called the doctor immediately as directed. He told her to get to the nearest hospital and they would know what to do. At the time we didn't know what that entailed, but now we do. There is no real sign of a low white blood cell count occurring. Only blood analysis can determine that. In fact, the day before Kris got the fever she mentioned that it was the first time since the chemo that she felt normal. So now even good days are suspect.

Did you know that we have 5 types of white blood cells in our bodies? Each has a specific job, with the neutrophil's job being to fight bacteria. With a low neutrophil count infections sprouted up all over her body. The infections were not from anyone bringing bacteria to her, e.g. from spreading their illness, rather, from the bacteria that is normally in our bodies. With such a low neutrophil count the bacteria that is normally kept in check had a big party and partied big time. Most of the infections were painful, but not life threatening, but the infection in her small intestine was life threatening. However, after 6 days in the hospital, a lot of antibiotics which are still continuing at home, white blood cell boosters, and excellent medical care she survived and is back home. Did you know (yes.....another 'did you know'....) that you can live without most of your large intestine, and without some of your small intestine, but if they have to remove too much of your small intestine you die? I didn't get a definition of what 'too much' is------------by the time I got all this info I was going into shock myself...... The purpose of the small intestine is the chemical digestion of food and absorption of nutrients into the blood. Without enough intestine to do this job you die due to lack of nutrition----your body starves to death. Kris was soooo scarily close to having surgery to remove part of the small intestine.

The Chemo doctor at Sloan Kettering told her at her first visit to him that things will be worse as the months progress------she will have chemo for about 9 months. I can't imagine how much worse things could possibly get. This first (and, I can only hope and pray, last) episode has delayed her scheduled chemo, something I hoped would not happen. We won't know when she will have the second treatment until Nov 21st when she goes back to Sloan.

Please keep up the prayers and good thoughts. She can use each and every one of them............... and little Owen is doing fine and makes his mom smile a lot----------which is his job and he does it well.

bless you all,

Claudia

RE: Update on Kristen

To Mom
From: Kimberly Perone
Sent: Mon 11/17/08 3:05 PM

Mom, wasn't it her large intestine that was in jeopardy?
Another quick question - might this be too much detail for your whole dept?

Remember when you told me not to talk too much after Jack died? That I'd go into too much detail when people asked me how I was. Stress, grief and worry can lead any of us into talking too much – it's therapeutic and helps us work things out. So no criticism here! Just constructive stuff. I Love you.

She's going to make it through all of this and this time next year we go on a destination Thanksgiving to celebrate!!!! Let's start planning - where should we go????

Kim

RE: Update on Kristen

To Kimberly Perone
From: mom
Sent: Mon 11/17/08 3:55 PM

my TI team is about 20 people.

no not large intestine. large is low this was high and the small intestine upper bowel near her appendix.
this was my short version not going into much detail..................but that is me................i figure it may make my peeps pray harder....................

Claudia

Brenda, who was also on the email distribution list, thought that perhaps the TMI (too much information) would lead to people worry about Mom's mental state. In response to my message above, I reported back to Brenda on the following lesson I learned.

RE: Update on Kristen

To Brenda
From:Kimberly Perone
Sent:Tue 11/18/08 3:08 PM

her response was....that was my short message. That way I have more of my peeps pray for Kris.

Moral - no matter how good you are, you can't give your parents advice.

LOL

Fw: Update on Kris

To Kimberly Perone
From: Brenda
Sent: Tues 5/05/09 4:25 PM

FYI. Not sure if you made the list.
Brenda

    <original message>

Subject: Update on Kris

To: Team TI
From: Claudia
Date: 05/05/09 3:50 PM

    As you know Kris had Brain Surgery on March 17th, however, although I have spoken with a few of you individually, I haven't communicated with my full email list since that time on her progress.

    In early April, she has completed the radiation (5 days of about an hour a day which included the set up and take down so the radiation itself was not the full hour). In late April she had her first of what I refer to as the 'last five' chemos. The second of the 'last five' should be late this week or early next. She'll find out at her appointment today with the chemo doctor.

    We had a major scare before the radiation began. Kris started having headaches again. Once you have had brain surgery a headache takes on a whole new meaning.......... The tumor that was left in was doubling in size every week. Although another brain surgery would probably be the best course it was ruled out because the doctors (who work as a team) felt that delaying chemo was a bigger risk. They felt that the radiation would still take care of the brain tumor, and then the long overdue chemo could start a week after radiation was complete.

The radiation happened, the waiting period ended, and the chemo started. At the time she had the chemo she started complaining of headaches again so they did an MRI. Her main doctors were out of town but the neurologist on call that ordered the MRI gave her the results. The tumor was larger and probably the cause of the headaches. The neurologist told Kris that the results would be given to her doctors and they would probably want to see her right away. This was on a Saturday and she had to wait till Monday to speak with one of the doctors on the team. It seemed like time was just standing still.

She spoke with the brain surgeon on Monday afternoon and he explained to her that the radiation itself can cause swelling, and therefore, headaches, and that was probably what was happening, rather than the tumor getting so large it was pushing on the nerves. He also explained that radiation keeps working after the sessions are over, therefore, they could not say---- just yet ----that the radiation was not working. It would take up to 6 weeks after the last radiation treatment to make that determination. Now wouldn't you think a neurologist would know this and could have explained that to Kris???? All our panic was washed away with that one important phone conversation..................

In addition to all the brain tumor issues (as if that weren't enough), we found out that what they felt were harmless 'nodes' in her lungs from all the infections she got with the neutropenic fever from the first chemo were actually harmful Ewing's tumors----
------6 of them. But the good news is that the chemo used to insure the leg tumor was gone gone gone has killed 3 of the lung tumors. The bad news is that 3 are still alive, with one growing faster than the

others. The doctor explained to Kris that when cancer branches out it may change DNA, just like family. Uncle Phil may look like Dad, but he has different DNA. So the 3 that are still alive may be mutations and need a different chemo..............but the good news here is that they have different chemo treatments, so if they need to adjust the chemo they can.

-As it stands now the headaches have subsided (thank God), and she is doing great. The radiation must be working.

-Chemo will begin again very soon. We originally were told that there would be 5 chemo treatments after the leg surgery, but that was before the brain tumors and brain surgery----------so we are really not sure how many more chemo's she'll have.

- A follow up see how well the radiation has worked is scheduled for May 14th (sooner than normal because of the occurrence of headaches).

- A follow up to see how the chemo is working on the lungs will probably happen the end of May.

When the results of the radiation and chemo are in we should know what Kris is facing for the near future. The up side is that the worst case scenario would be surgery on the brain again, and/ or lungs to remove the tumors. More chemo treatments with the same or different drugs are also possibilities. The very best we can hope for, and we are hoping and praying for, is that the brain scan will show the radiation has killed the one live brain tumor and that no more tumors of the brain are detected, and that the MRI of the lungs will show those last 3 tumors are also dead with no signs of other lung tumors.

Even if we get the best news it still means years of follow-up------which is very much welcomed. This type of cancer likes to pop up again and again and again anywhere in the body................the earlier detected the earlier the fight can begin. The earlier the fight the better the chances of winning. I guess you could say 'life is war'.

Take care and keep up the great prayers...........
God Bless
Claudia

No, I didn't make the list anymore. I had been cut off. I was taken off the list for having insinuated that Mom could perhaps summarize more. When the subject came up with Mom later, she said to me, "Of course you are off the list!"

And a few moments later,

"And if I _hear_ _that_ _Brenda_ is sending you the emails, she's off the list too!!!!" I think she may have sneered at me, too. *Okay, momma bear.*

I kept Brenda's emails to me top secret until now.

The Blue Elephant in the Room

In 2009, Steven came home with a remarkable art project. It was a large paper Mache elephant. Painted entirely bright royal blue, the only part that was not perfectly proportioned was the trunk. It was a little thin and flat on the face, but perfect at its peanut end. Dave and I both love it. Sure, we are his parents, but this was a real accomplishment. It stands two feet high and ten inches wide. It is like a sculpture in our house. Today, the elephant stands proudly at the top of the bookshelf in our family room, watching protectively over its creator who is playing video games and entertaining friends.

When Steven first brought him home, I tried to find the perfect place so the world could see. I settled on the side table in the dining room. Our living room and dining room are connected without walls. There, from his corner, our blue elephant can see visitors as they walked into the front door.

After some time in this spot, I mentioned the elephant in the room and it stopped me in my tracks. Hey, the elephant in the room! How funny. Pleased with the art, its placement, and the play on words, I told Mom and Kristen about it when we were in Connecticut.

"When you come to my house you'll have to look at the elephant in the room. But we don't like to talk about him!"

Mom corrected me, "That's the *800-pound gorilla in the corner.*"

"I don't think so," I said.

"It's the *white* elephant in the room," Kristen added.

Again, I shook my head no, while swallowing my mouthful of cheese and cracker, picking up my glass of wine. "They all mean things, I mean, they are all real *expressions,* but they all refer to different things," I said.

"No, I still think it is the 800-pound gorilla," Mom said.

We chuckled, and someone must have walked in the room and changed the topic. So with the conversation unfinished, we all stood in our own *corner of the room* on which expression was the right one—the one that means an obvious truth that is being ignored or a risk that no one will acknowledge and discuss.

Back at home, I see our friendly elephant. This reminds me, I need to Google all the elephant expressions. Just as I thought, the 800-pound gorilla is the big fish in your pond, to use a more familiar expression. For the Computer Shack, it would be Dell, for Andy's Hardware, it is Home Depot. A white elephant, which is *not* followed by 'in the corner' or 'in the room,' is something big and expensive that you are trying to get rid of—a useless building, for example—whose maintenance cost exceeds its worth. As for my elephant in the room, we don't like to talk about him, but I'll make an exception here.

A month later, my sister came to visit for the weekend. Since she started chemotherapy it had been easier for us to go to her in Connecticut, rather than for them to make the three-hour trek with the baby to New York. We were excited that she could spend some time at home. Her former home. She was able to stay at Dad's house. Everyone got a chance to see her. It had been a while since our neighbors at camp, some of them like family, had seen Kristen.

Kim Perone

Probably not since her wedding two years prior. And definitely not since Owen was born and her cancer diagnosis four months later.

Now they got to see Kris and baby Owen. She looked great. She wore a scarf to cover her bald head, mostly not to sunburn. She lacked any vanity and was beautiful and glowing. Her skin was pale, but smooth and flawless like porcelain. People flowed in and out, visiting and talking about old times, when we were all younger running around at camp.

When it was time for Owen's nap, I gladly took him inside and told my sister to continue visiting. It was a point in my life where I had limited ability to make small talk. I was overusing the skill in my 'hi-how-are-ya hi-how-are-ya' job in public relations and devoting much energy to keeping a brave face. We all were. She was enjoying the socializing so much I felt less guilt about hiding from friends and family.

She beamed with pride, showing off her little boy, and now enjoyed time to visit without trying to entertain or chase after him. Danielle, Kristen's friend since birth, was there with her own children and parents. Danielle's father has been our father's best friend since high school and he and his wife are Kristen's godparents.

A few days before, I had finally gotten the courage to talk to my cousin, an oncologist in Florida. It was a conversation I had been avoiding for months, while we kept him posted at a safe distance with emails.

"What is happening?" I finally asked, sensing his trepidation. He told me. When pressed for a time estimate he reluctantly said she would not make it to New Year's Day 2010. I could hear him crying.

"It's so unfair," he sobbed.

It was August. I sat expressionless and completely still as if any movement would prove that this was a real moment. Unmoving, sitting on the couch listening to his sobs my limbs drained of all fluid. *Not again.*

"Soon you will need to talk to Krissy about end of life issues," he added.

As Kristen's visit was coming to an end, we took the customary group photos, placing the cameras on my fireplace mantel and arranging ourselves on the couch. We checked to see if the camera's auto-function worked. Next we moved out to the front yard and driveway continuing with our 40-minute family goodbye session. Today, there were tearful goodbyes, the hugs from Kristen longer.

"We'll be in Connecticut next week," I said. "Can't wait! Love you." Everyone piled into their cars and drove off as I waved. I could tell it was hard for her to leave.

When I walked back in the house the blue elephant in the room greeted me with his knowing eyes and silent accusations.

I know, but how? I just can't. I am not even sure if I should, I telepathically replied.

Letting go

For seven hours we sat in Kristen's room without talking to each other while she lay in the coma the doctor predicted would only last an hour. But she held on. She was always fighting and never complaining or giving up. I can't imagine the realization that you will not make it. That you will die. I only know the feeling of being told the person I love will not make it. Mom told me that Kristen said to her near the end, "I really thought I was going to make it," with a tone of questioning disbelief. We did, too.

After seven hours of waiting and watching every haggard breath, Nurse Jackie, a wonderful woman in her late 60s, thin and spry, with a take-charge attitude, who Kristen *adored*, told us that her body was fighting her. Her vegetarian, low weight, fit, strong, brave, well-other-than-cancer body was fighting her death even in a coma induced by the uncontrollable cancer in her lungs.

Beyond the horror at hand, I began to worry about Owen and relieving my brother-in-law's mother who was at the house watching the active and energetic 15-month-old. This could go on all night, I thought. I stepped out into the recreation lounge to collect my thoughts and understand my own mixed feelings of waiting anxiously for my sister to die and not wanting her to die. There was no way back and frankly, she had suffered enough. I know heaven is better than this torture of cancer and the modern medicine that fights it. We had watched her suffer enough. My parents had watched her suffer enough.

I went down in the elevator and started walking in the rain in my ratty sweatpants and frayed decade-old Cape Cod sweatshirt to find a place to go. *Somewhere other than the hospital, so I can breathe.* I found a deli with a salad bar. To know me is to know my love for salad. I like the relentless chewing a salad provides. I suppose since I felt like jumping out of my skin, aggressive chewing might be something to do. *How helpless are we? What else can I do?* My heart didn't need or want food, my anger needed it, but I hadn't eaten since I don't know when.

Back in the lounge on the 15th floor, with my takeout salad, I chewed and chewed angrily. This was the place where Kris and I made mosaic art as a desperate attempt to allay the anxiety that was overwhelming. It was also the place where we played the game of Clue on the outdoor deck while rubbing Kristen's legs and watching other families wheel their loved around to enjoy fresh air. The air of the rest of the world.

This needs to end. If the end is coming, let it come now. If I am waiting for the axe to fall, let it fall now. I am mad at the doctors. I am mad at their optimism and for not being up front with Kristen and Omar, so that she might have some ability for last thoughts, wishes. *Any wishes for a future that exists without her. For her baby. What does she want us to do? We can't ask now.*

In the past month in the hospital we tried to be so positive.

"You'll get out," we would say. Kristen's anxiety grew.

"I feel like I'll never get out of here," she told the hospital social worker. That was when she was coherent, yet with three tubes sticking out of her side to drain the lung fluid. We would walk the halls dragging the unit around. She said she felt like a monster.

A monster – she was far from it. My gorgeous, worldly, 34-

year-old sister. Long, light brown hair. Perfect teeth. Clear blue eyes. Thin and beautiful. Vital. Vegetarian. Healthy. A Rensselaer Polytechnic Institute chemical engineering graduate, with an MBA. Her climb up the ladder was well marked and accelerating. She was certainly on the executive track, widely respected by her peers, loved by her superiors. She traveled the world, had a picture-perfect wedding, tons of friends, and a sophisticated Connecticut life.

And now there was even a little boy. A handsome little redheaded baby. All of her life-long dreams had fallen into place like a puzzle. Owen was four months old when she was diagnosed.

Life wrecked out of the blue. Out of nowhere.

I remember sitting with her on her bed as she contemplated her first chemo treatment, afraid of not being able to take care of Owen. Her long wet hair was dripping onto her tank top, making dark blue splotches. She was holding her hair brush in her hand, reminding me that all her beautiful hair would be gone a month from now. Her legs in pajama bottoms, curled tight to her body as she dejectedly leaned on the pillows behind her. Tears rolled down her face.

"I'm scared of not being able to take care of Owen," she choked out. I am not sure if she was referring to the short term or long term.

"We are here for you...Think of us as your arms and legs..." *You are our priority. Do not worry.* I was convinced we would see her through this. *We will get through this.*

The months that followed were a courageous battle. Mom and I were around as much as possible. She never doubted her ability to persevere. This day at the hospital, three weeks into her stay and the eleventh month of her cancer, every day was a combination of pain and fear. The "you'll-leave-tomorrow" messages became a daily conversation.

"Not today, tomorrow," doctors and nurses would say, and we would echo.

Tomorrow would never come. Today was the tomorrow that would never come.

Ever growing in her anxiousness and pain, my sister's pain-killers were increased and increased to the point that she was incoherent. A relief and loss. She was stripped of her ability to do anything more than ask for the drink on the table, then the Thick-It on the table. That stupid cup of water and thickening solution, called Thick-It, which makes water like applesauce so that people choking on growing tumors can swallow their liquid.

Everyone was scared to talk about what was happening or ask my sister any questions. She wasn't anxious anymore, she was just spaced out.

Back in the lounge on the last day, the last hours, I stabbed my fork into the remainders in the disposable container, my mother joined me.

"I think I need to go to the house. This could go on all night," I handed her the fork. She poked at the marinated mozzarella ball in the plastic container. As she continued to push around the lone grape tomato with the fork, she agreed with me.

"I know," she said and looked up at the ceiling with her fists balled "Kristen Marie Percent Mureebe, let go!"

It was a mother's message. Mother's love. Mother's orders. Mother's greatest fear. Release yourself from this pain and agony. Go toward the light and find eternal peace.

After all, hadn't I done the same thing five years ago?

Whether from obedience, a promise of peace, or permission, Mom was heard. A minute later, we were beckoned. "You need to come back now."

We entered the room knowing without needing to be told that Kristen stopped breathing. I'll never forget the image of my brother-in-law and my father, seated on either side and leaning over Kristen in perfect symmetry; my mother and me, coming into the room in perfect symmetry.

The cancer was done with its destruction. It won. Nature would do the rest. We would begin to believe the unbelievable, and grieve to our core.

Kim Perone

Nanny Ba-Nanny

When I was expecting my first child, my mom was pondering her nickname preference. Did she want to be Grandma, Granny, Grammy, anything else...? After hours and days, maybe months, of thoughtful consideration, she chose none of the above. She chose Nanny because she figured the "N" sound would come out before the "G" sound. She was also forty-three years old, young by today's standards for grandmas. So before her competitor, my mother-in-law, took Nanny she reserved the name. And of course, my mother-in-law was already Grandma to all the other grandkids. At the time, my nieces and nephews ranged in ages from ten years old to twenty, three girls and three boys. My baby was the tie breaker.

On October 20, 1994 Jonathon Angelo Perone was born. Jonathon, so he had a formal name for the sake of it and we could call him Jack, the real name choice; and Angelo in memory of my husband's paternal grandfather. It was a long labor (a bit similar to my own birth), over 24 hours before he made his grand appearance. And it *was* grand. If I could sell that feeling, the one that comes after giving birth, then all other drugs would cease to exist in lieu of the "I just had a baby" drug. It is the most magnificent and glorious of all feelings I have ever had in my life. The entire world stops. And of course, the pain does also, so that is a major plus and no doubt, adds to the euphoria. I have to watch myself when talking with a group of women if there is one among them who has not yet had this experience. I used to always temper myself around Kristen.

My memory of labor—the pain and violence of it—is still quite strong, although many women do not have that same experience. But the glorious, magnificent, I-just-became-a-mom-and-everything-is-okay-and-nothing-else-in-the-world-matters-at-all-feeling is one I'll cherish my whole life along with my son.

Needless to even say, Jonathon Angelo—Jack—was adored by everyone. On my side he was the first grandchild. On Dave's side, he was a baby among teenagers so everyone, including his cousins, enjoyed having a little one around again.

My father was dating my future stepmother, Rena, and she was there to enjoy Jack from the very beginning. Within the next few years, my mother would be set up on a blind date with Dan and he would soon become a permanent member of the family. One that my mother reminds me is temporary, so he knows that if he gets out of line (her line, that is) he's gone. To this day, she has him pay rent so that she can evict him if necessary. (Over-corrective post-divorce control.) He is so permanent; she just won't dare admit it!

Dan also loved Jack. He had a nine-year-old son at the time and soon we would be introducing our little Jack to the Jets as the hand-me-down memorabilia flowed generously to our house.

As it turns out, I think Jack actually pronounced his "g" sounds first, but whatever. It isn't a popularity contest, right? Each grandmother had her own special relationship with Jack. My mother-in-law babysat three days per week when I worked. Jack and Nanny had a very close relationship. Mom was always there, and as my mother, the most trusted of all. She was the first to babysit him at all, the first to take care of him overnight, and the first to make projects with him.

Nanny and Jack spent New Year's Eve 1994 together.

Nanny and Jack dressed up in red, white, and blue outfits for Fourth of July.

Nanny and Jack went to Hoffman's Playland.

Nanny and Jack created painted planets for a universe mobile.

Nanny and Jack went to Broadway shows and museums in New York City.

Nanny and Jack went to baseball games—Go Yankees.

Nanny and Jack were on the go; they had people to see, places to go.

When Steve was born, Mom came to stay overnight. I was sick with a head cold, Steve was about two weeks old, and Dave had just fallen off a ladder changing a light on the front of our house, cracking his elbow on the cement steps. They didn't cast the elbow so he was in constant pain. He could not even pick up baby Stevie and forget doing anything with two-year-old Jack. I was so sick and so very tired. I needed my mommy! *Nanny to the rescue!*

As Steve grew, she started taking the both boys to her house overnight. It was a handful but she could do it. She did, however, get to the point where she wanted them solo. "They play with each other and not me!" she said.

She didn't want to just have them at the house. She had an agenda. She had plans in mind, things she wanted to do, projects to make, trips, and it was better one-on-one. It was Nanny Palooza.

So we started alternating overnight visits to Nanny's house, allowing her to savor her time with each of them. The boys enjoyed their alone time and yet also missed each other. Steve especially missed Jack. Jack was his idol. He was the little brother and Jack was the captain. He was "mission control." He was the leader for everything they did. He knew how to pop in a video or start a game.

Steve was the ball kind of kid, always with a ball of some sort, kicking, throwing, bopping, and shooting hoops. No interest in books or Legos—that was Jack's territory.

Mom recounted the ball pit story for us after a trip to McDonald's with Steve when he was two. "This kid was in there, maybe six years old, and he started throwing balls right at Steve, but he kept missing so I didn't say anything. Then Steve started throwing back and bam, bam, bam. 1, 2, 3, right between the eyes! I was going to stop it, but that kid started it. What was I going to do, tell Steve he's too good and should stop picking on a kid three times his age?"

These days she and I both sigh when it comes to fourteen-year-old Steve and his lack of interest in doing things with us. What can we do? He is a normal teenage boy. At least we have shopping. When there is a big ticket electronic item that he wants, we are 'all that'. But other than that, you can see he can't relate to us. He would rather be playing his Xbox.

But now we have Owney Baloney to cuddle and play with, thankfully. I see Nanny with Owen and it really brings me back in time. She is Nanny Ba-Nanny and he is Owney Baloney. Owen adores his Nanny, just as Jack and Steven did. We spend a lot of time with Owen. When he was a newborn, she created the Owen song,

> Lit-tle Ow-en Mur-ah-bee,
> The cutest little baby you ever did see,
> a-b-c-d-e- f-g,
> Lit-tle Ow-en Mur-ah-bee.

Kim Perone

He always smiled, stopped crying, or went to sleep when he heard his little song. In fact, as he got older I used the song to get him to smile for the camera. He was always looking at me with this blank expression when I was trying to take a photo. I started singing the song and he would look at me and smile. *Click.*

Six years ago, Nanny and Jack did finish their work of art in 2004. The universe mobile, was finally completed the year Jack died. They worked on it for five years! Nanny said, "We need to hurry up and finish before they discover another planet!"

She took the idea from a project we did in Girl Scouts a thousand years prior. I think Mom and Jack started that when he was four. Mom has pictures of the different visits when Jack and she worked on that mobile. Mercury, Venus, Earth, Mars, Jupiter, Saturn, Uranus, Neptune, and Pluto. Rather than discovering another planet, Pluto was downgraded to a dwarf planet in a 2006 decision, according to the following Wikipedia excerpt (see url below).

"*Main article: Definition of planet*

The definition of *planet* set in 2006 by the International Astronomical Union (IAU) states that in the Solar System a planet is a celestial body that:

1.   is in orbit around the Sun,

2. has sufficient mass to assume hydrostatic equilibrium (a nearly round shape), and

3. has "cleared the neighbourhood" around its orbit.

A non-satellite body fulfilling only the first two of these criteria is classified as a "dwarf planet". According to the IAU, "planets and dwarf planets are two distinct classes of objects". A non-satellite body fulfilling only the first criterion is termed a "small solar system body" (SSSB). Initial drafts planned to include dwarf planets as a subcategory of planets, but because this could potentially have led to the addition of several dozens of planets into the Solar System, this draft was eventually dropped. In 2006, it would only have led to the addition of three (Ceres, Eris and Makemake) and the reclassification of one (Pluto). The definition was a controversial one and has drawn both support and criticism from different astronomers, but has remained in use.

According to the definition, there are currently eight planets and five dwarf planets known in the Solar System. The definition distinguishes planets from smaller bodies and is not useful outside the Solar System, where smaller bodies cannot be found yet. Extrasolar planets, or exoplanets, are covered separately under a complementary 2003 draft guideline for the definition of planets, which distinguishes them from dwarf stars, which are larger.

http://www.ask.com/wiki/IAU_definition_of_planet?qsrc=3044 (date: January 26, 2011)

Kim Perone

Jack

In 2004, back in town from our Cape Cod vacation, the boys needed to get the last of their school items. Our last, and possibly the most important item, was yet to be purchased—Jack's sneakers. He had a very specific idea this year. Black converse high tops. This was something totally different from his usual skater shoes.

When we were on vacation, I remember passing the sneaker outlet a number of times, but thought, why spend a moment shopping when we can do that at home. Each time we passed, I almost mentioned it to Dave, but thought better of it. So after vacation and after work on a Tuesday, the boys and I set off to buy sneakers. Jack was nine, Stevie seven.

As we left the house, I was trying to figure out which mall to go to—three were equal distance from our house. I picked a direction and we headed off to the mall. The time was about 5:40 PM. We drove up past our house, crossed over Snakehill Road, and continued up Closson Road where my father-in-law lived.

"Wave to Papa," I said as we passed.

At the hill, a left and quick right down Rector Road, a steep hill ending at Route 5. I often took this path to go to the plant in Rotterdam Junction. At the time, I worked as a public relations manager for a family-owned chemical company. Although I worked at the headquarters at one end of the county, I often traveled for meetings to the manufacturing site, which was located just off of Route 5. I waited at the stop sign at end of Rector Road. It was a sunny and gorgeous day. Life was good.

"Mom, Steven's falling asleep," Jack said.

He knew to say that because I had warned the kids about the back airbags on the side next to the window. I had read in the car's manual that rear side air bags can kill a child if their head is leaning on it when it deploys. So the kids were continually reminded to lean toward the center rather than the door.

In response to Jack's warning, I said in a singsong voice "Stev-ie, lean toward the middle. We're almost there." He groggily obliged. It was a long wait for an opening in the traffic. We were patient. A rust-colored car took a right turn into the road we were on at the time, giving me an opening to take a left. I accelerated. A ghost of a truck popped up on my left side. I tried to get across the lane faster.

"Oh shit!" I said, as I pushed the gas pedal as hard as I could.

When my eyes opened, I was looking out of my broken windshield at the grass on the other side of the road. Realizing what had happened my legs started pumping and I grabbed the door handle to jump out. It wouldn't open. Fighting panic, I looked back to see Jack leaning over unconscious. He was bleeding from his left temple. A voice, *my own voice,* far above me calmly said, "They might tell me my children are dead right now."

I looked to the right and saw Steven staring at me wide-eyed through mangled glasses. I reached into my purse and pulled out my cell phone. Any other time it would have taken me ten minutes to find it. But not now, it was right there. I hit redial for Dave.

"Come quick...I have been in an accident...Route 5."

After being cut out of the car, I was put on a stretcher and only remember looking up and seeing Dave standing over me. He said I was screaming, "Where's Jack!?" Steven was on a stretcher also and we were loaded into the ambulance. Dave told me Jack was going in a helicopter to Albany Medical Center. Steven and I stared at each other in fear, holding hands over a bloodied Happy Meal frog. The ride seemed to take forever. It was surreal. Dave was driven by the policeman to the hospital.

In the emergency room, no one would tell me how Jack was. Steven was now with Dave, having had his broken finger wrapped and the gash on his head stapled, otherwise, he was fine, thankfully. Dave looked down at me still on a stretcher and asked if he should call Mom.

Yes.

Dad.

Yes.

Brenda.

Yes.

People streamed in, but my focus was solely on the doctors and who was going to tell me how Jack was.

"He is over there. We'll know more later," the doctor said.

I was consciously pushing the panic down deep inside me. I was calm and spoke calmly to the staff.

None of this is real. It can't be. Before I left work I packed up the speech for tomorrow evening's going away party for my work friend, Dawn. It is all arranged. She is leaving the company to go to Hawaii with her husband and little girls. I need to be there tomorrow. I need to give the speech. It is so funny. Lots of Hawaii jokes. This isn't happening. Of course this isn't happening.

The policeman took a breathalyzer and showed me the zero on

the monitor. He said it was customary procedure. As I lay on the emergency room bed, I continued to focus on not panicking and seeing Jack's face again.

Arrival of Mom

Mom.

Mom arrived at the hospital and when I saw her I knew everything would be okay. I pushed down the panic.

I was still on a stretcher in the emergency room. As I looked at her, I pushed the panic down further. Down.

I was getting calmer. I was staying calm.

"They won't tell me about Jack," I said.

Her lips were moving, but I don't know what she said. The room was swirling around me. *Mom's here so it will be okay, she'll find out.*

Steve was with Dave in another room.

I closed my eyes for a moment.

Dave and Steven will go home soon.

As much as we did not want to separate our family, I wanted Dave with Steven and Steve out of the hospital. Mom stayed with me.

I was moved to a 'parent room' in the Pediatric Intensive Care Unit. There was a bed with a nightstand. A phone. A bathroom.

Mom brought me clothes – sweatpants and shirt, socks, sneakers. I had been wearing a summer dress and flip flops. It doesn't seem appropriate anymore.

I dressed and looked at my face in the mirror. Other than cuts on the side of my face, I was fine. But I hurt everywhere inside and out.

I want to hold my breath and stop time and go back. Rewind. Maybe this is a dream, a nightmare. It cannot be happening for real.

I was led down the hall to Jack's bedside. Finally, I got to see Jack.

He was in bed connected to many machines. It didn't look like him. He was unconscious.

I met the nurse. We talked.

The nurse explained that they were monitoring Jack for brain swelling. They put him in a chemically induced coma to decrease brain stimulation. I could sit in a chair and watch him. We dim the lights.

I prayed.

The next day, Dave came back and my father picked up Steven. He was to stay with Dad and Rena at camp. Kristen and Omar arrived. They would also stay at camp with Steven.

Dave and I now stay at the hospital along with my mother. She is our arms and legs. If we need anything she will go get it. We take turns sitting by Jack's side as the hours and days pass. Only one of us at a time is allowed. We need to wave our hand over the security unit by the door. They ask who we are. Jonathon's mom. Jonathon's dad. *Only then, can we go in to see Jack.*

During Dave's time by the bedside, he came out, desperate and asking for my mother. "He is getting worse, the swelling, and I can't, can't be in there because I have negative energy and your mother -- she has to go in there because it's bad. She is positive, positive energy. Get her and tell her to go in. Now!" He stumbled into the parent room and sat down on the bed.

She went in and held vigil over Jack. We were trying to keep the stimulation low. Darkness. Quiet. Whoever wasn't in there tried to deflect visitors to the hospital. They couldn't be there, but because no one was getting information they just showed up. Balloons, cards, stuffed animals – from kids at school and the Y. The baseball team. Dave's fellow coach's wife and a dear friend, brought me a book of Psalms. I read them when I was sitting with Jack. *God, my heart is pure. Make this okay, I trust in you.*

Over and over.

Brenda helped to communicate to the outside world.

In the middle of the night, I called four of my closest work-friends' desk phones. I left messages saying that I was sure everything would be alright.

By the end of the third day, we finally saw a doctor for the first time since we arrived, the neurosurgeon from the ER, where he had said to me, "We are monitoring Jack" but refused to say more than "you look very calm." I had replied, "I am pushing the panic down." *Not because any of this is even vaguely okay. Not because I don't care. But because I can't do anything to go back in time and go in another direction.*

He said that over these three days they had assessed the situation, and then, calmly and unemotionally told us the worst thing we could hear. "Jack is as hurt as a boy can be. He suffered a traumatic brain stem injury in the accident."

Our bodies went slack. He told us that surgery would relieve the swelling inside Jack's skull, but that Jack, *our Jack,* would survive in a vegetative state.

Through the grace of God, Dave and I knew what we needed

to do and did not need to debate or discuss. We knew what Jack would want.

Luckily, Mom wasn't there at the time to hear this with us. She returned after researching brain trauma. We sat her down and told her that Jack was not coming back to us. I pet her hair, while Dave and I held her from each side, sobs wracking her body. *No. No. No. No.* Rocking back and forth.

Mom was the first of many people we told.

Butterfly, Butterfly, Fly Away Home

Believe like your life depends on it. Mine did.

> For God so loved the world that He gave His only begotten Son, so that everyone who believes in Him will not perish but have eternal life.

> — John 3:16 (New International Version)

It is an inscription I chose for Jack's headstone.

In the days that followed his death, I was among other things, teetering on the edge of sanity. I was falling and scared and could easily have taken my own life. But I do believe. And if I ever forget to believe, I was going to need reminders to tell me to hang on to life so that I might see Jack. Believe that he believed as well. He believed and therefore, he has eternal life. *That's how this works, right?*

The panic in me roared through the false calm, building into a scream that I silenced before it escaped and I fell into darkness. The nightmare was real.

By my side during all of this was my mother. She sat with me while I planned the funeral. We sent Dave with Steve to pick out his birthday present. An unusual task on such a day, I realize, but nevertheless a task that needed doing. Again, I wanted them to stay together while Mom and I handled this horrific task.

Mom sat with me as I picked out a casket, as we together wrote the obituary of a fifth grader we loved. Mom sat with me as I was shown gravesites and headstone options. "Sat with me" doesn't begin to describe it. She shepherded me there. She was the leader in our sad, sad parade.

Months later, maybe even a year later or two later, she said, "You are the strongest person I know... *besides me.*" While I smiled internally at the double-edged compliment, I realized how very true it is. She is a rock. She has been my rock for as long as I can remember.

No horror can break her. She helped us through the loss of Jack and was by my sister's side during her losing battle with cancer five years later. No tragedy, no setback, no *nothing* can stop us. When Dave sings jokingly (and lovingly, I might add), "I am woman hear me roar...." a line from that old Helen Reddy song, he refers to us. It always makes me laugh.

But more than that, Mom is a survivor.

For whatever reason I dare not ponder, we have each lost a child. *Why must we share the same tragedy, the loss of a child?* I realize that this may not be as statistically rare as it seems, but I believe that every family and every person has their own path and their own obstacles. I would be the last to say our story is *more* sad than any other. But ours does seem to be the type movies are made of: the sudden accidental death of a child; the disease and the death of a young mother who is also a child. No second chance recovery. No near miss. No almost.

Today, our solidarity exists not only in the similarity of our looks, our laughter, or our personalities, but it also lies in our spirits, in our survival and grief.

Kim Perone

My mother always said, "I am not your friend. I am your mother. You have friends." While we do lots of fun things together—more and more over the years as we get older—she has never believed that mothers and daughters should be friends. She is my mother and there is a difference.

Now that I am an adult, our relationship is much beyond mother-daughter or friendship. She is the strongest person I know. And I am the strongest person she knows, *besides her.* We are not contemporaries, there is a hierarchy. There is a wisdom and strength that I *need* her to have, a wisdom and strength beyond mine. She is always older, wiser, and I can only hope that when it comes to our deaths, we go in the order nature intended. Although it would not surprise me one bit if she lived to be a hundred. And if she did live that long, there is a good chance she would lose her other daughter as well.

Mom believes in fate. She believes that Kristen's rare cancer and the even more rare chance that someone in her demographic ended up with it, is a sign to her that it was meant to be. Kristen's case was one in a million. Her cancer only affects around 300 people per year and of those people, almost all are between 18-25 year old males. For whatever reason, she was supposed to leave us at thirty-four.

I believe that Jack gave me signs. Our souls knew. I dreamt of his death a few months before our accident. While the scenario was different, the crashing glass in the dream was the same. He told me of his homework assignment which was to write about what you most feared and at nine years old, he wrote about his fear of dying. I asked him, "Why would you be afraid of dying?" and he said, "Isn't everyone?" Maybe his soul knew he would die before his next birthday.

After talking to many grieving parents, I realize we all have our signs, our warning dreams, and our beliefs. These signs and beliefs help us cling to a world in which we no longer want to live, when carrying the scar of a child's death. These signs and beliefs enable us to function, to continue on until our own lives end.

All of this also makes my mother's humor so important to me. The fact that we can still laugh, and that our laughter buoys us, is a small miracle.

One summer day, when I had taken my two-year-old nephew, Owen, to the beach, a gorgeous orange butterfly circled him. The butterfly would not leave and kept flitting around his face, then landed on the sand. Owen was a bit scared of the thick creature with colorful wings, wings that matched his own hair and swim shorts. The breeze was pushing against the butterfly wherever it landed. I thought something might be wrong with the butterfly. *Why would she hang onto the sand, only leaping from one place to another place rather than fly away?* Especially with us surrounding her.

Why? Because she was saying hello. My sister was saying hello. Hello to her son. She sat on his shoulder and then floated to the sand. He examined her with trepidation. She stayed as long as she could, until she was satisfied. Satisfied that he was okay and had also said hello. *All my love, little one.* Then, just as suddenly as she appeared, she left us.

Butterfly, butterfly, fly away home.

Are there hardwood floors in heaven?

I was talking to my mother about my decision to resign from my job. I explained that since Kristen passed away, I am even more aware of how fragile life is, even after all we had already been through. We work so hard for tomorrow or later and frankly, there might not be a later.

She thoroughly agreed. In fact, she said, matter-of-factly, "That is why I am putting in hardwood floors. There might not *be* hardwood floors in heaven." Very dry humor.

Most people use the expression "out of the mouths of babes," but for me, it is out of the mouth of my mother. Yet again, she keeps laughing. No reason to stop now.

In the aftermath of my sister's death, our dark humor buoyed our spirit to keep it from drowning. If you do not hang onto that piece of driftwood in the ocean you may not make it to shore. The driftwood is the humor you find in the incredulous, ridiculous, and unfair loss of a once healthy loved one. It is not funny. But it is okay to survive and cherish your most prized quality—your spirit—while your loved one enters the afterlife.

Before Kristen passed, we traded places day in and day out, at the hospital and at the house, caring for her and my infant nephew. We saw the situation grow increasingly bleak. We knew the horrible reality of what was about to come. When we were all comforting each other months later, my mother said, "I wanted to tell her to go toward the light."

Somehow, I found this funny. "Mom, where did you think she would go?" I asked.

Then I realized that those books we read after Jack's death *do* mention that people are torn between the afterlife and their earthly life. Although, they are normally torn in the *opposite* direction. They say they did want to go toward the light. They did not want to come back. They felt drawn to eternal life and whatever that feels like. It feels good, I think, beyond words even. But Kristen had so much to hang on for, especially a life with Owen. If we would lay our lives down for our children, we must certainly cling to life for them as well. That's why Mom wanted to tell her to go *toward* the light.

My response to Mom's comment was simple, perhaps even comforting. "Don't worry, Kristen's a smart woman. I am sure she knew just what to do. I mean, she has an MBA for goodness sake!"

In fact, at the point she let go and went toward the light, I pictured my sister smiling, looking down from above with all the symbols of her healthy self, returned to her—her long wavy hair and beautiful figure—looking at peace from our ceiling and the floor of heaven, rubbing her bare feet on the smooth *hardwood floor? Tile floor? Marble? Yes*...marble floor; and waving and saying, "See you later!" *See you in the next life.*

That is my image anyway.

Men are Stupid

The snow just keeps on coming. Here in upstate New York, the winters are long, dry, gray, and complicated. Our snow banks are already four feet high and the meteorologist is predicting 5-9 inches more. If we are lucky we get a little freezing rain. It makes the roads tough, but doesn't add height. Today is Groundhog Day 2011 and apparently Punxsutawney Phil did not see his shadow. This means an early spring. He always sees his shadow. This is encouraging.

"I called Aunt Janney, but I didn't get an answer," Mom says. "She is traveling to Joey's before flying to Tennessee with him to visit her in-laws. I wonder if the snow changed their plans. I guess your cousin feels like his grandparents don't have much time left so he wanted to plan a trip to visit. I can't believe they are still alive. She's had cancer and other things and seems to keep going along. Sometimes I wonder if it is a punishment or reward."

I agree. Since the loss of Jack and Kristen, I, too, wonder if the good die young and those of us who need to work on things get to keep living this seemingly good life and suffering its upsets and disappointments.

"Mom, remember when I called you and said that Dave asked me if I loved him?

"Yes, I do," she says.

It was Mother's Day 2006. Although nearly two years had

passed since Jack's death, chronic emotional pain was our daily companion. We spent our Saturday nights playing cards with our best friends Brenda, Paul, and Dave B.

We had settled into a comfortable and safe routine, found a way to have fun without being in public. My husband has always had the ability to drink large quantities of beer and we have the stories to prove it—like when he fell backward off the picnic table in what looked like slow motion. My capacity for drinking was new. In grief, alcohol provides a numbness that is desirable. For the first time in my life, I became someone who had a hard time stopping.

One Saturday night we had cards at our house. Steve, who was now ten years old, was staying at a friend's overnight. I always felt relieved when he was at a friend's house and away from our tense and sad household. We did our best to make our family life normal, but he saw more than his fair share of sadness and drunkenness.

Since he was away, I let go. Since it was Mother's Day weekend, I was hurting. Birthdays and Mother's Day just are not the same after your child dies. They are reminders of your loss and failure. I never knew how much I liked vodka. I drank about eight mandarin orange vodka and diet tonics. I filled my short glass to the brim, creating what has become a joke among friends.

"Kim, don't you think that's a little too full?" said Paul.

Brenda tells the story by saying in a high voice, "I'll get it," and raises her arms in the air while bending down to pretend slurp the top of the glass. I do remember doing that. We called it the meniscus (kneecap). The liquid was brimming over but holding on to the sides of the glass forming a bubble. It was like a convex meniscus, looming over the glass.

But after vodka tonics on top of a heavy heart I wasn't just hung-over, I was hung-over for *three days.* I was a disaster. Luckily, Steve was still hanging with friends the next day. Dave had left to help his brother with a household project. I called my mom to wish her a happy Mother's Day. Somehow I ended up crying.

Dave asked me if I loved him," I wept. "Why wouldn't he just tell me he loved me? Why is he asking me?!"

To me it was a sure sign he blamed me for Jack's death. He's not stupid.

"Men are stupid," Mom said.

"Not that stupid."

"Of *course*, they are that stupid!"

"Why wouldn't…" I was rolling on the floor of my bedroom.

"Yes, men really, truly are that stupid. You are having an anxiety attack from too much drink. You need fatty food and protein. Isn't it good you have a mother with a big drinking history?"

After some greasy food, peanut butter, and a couple of days to dry out, I was indeed glad to have a mother who knew these things.

A few months before that episode, I had started taking antidepressants on the advice of my doctor. I guess they hadn't quite kicked in yet. I had gone to the doctor sure it was low blood pressure. I was experiencing dizziness, extreme fatigue and tingling in my thighs. I was tired. When the nurse was making small talk with me while taking my blood pressure she asking what else might be making me tired.

"My ten year old sleeps with us."

She looked at me funny, and said "Why is your ten year old sleeping with you?" like 'you must be kidding.'

"Because his brother died and I told him he could sleep with us until he was forty."

She looked mortified. I started crying and could not get myself to stop. I kept trying to pull myself back together, while inside I was ready to fall on the ground and beg someone to kill me. In fact, as I write these words at this moment, I find myself sobbing, remembering the helplessness and hopelessness of that time. I had come undone.

When the doctor came in he asked me a few questions and told me I was not having a low blood pressure episode and that this—this person in front of him—was not me. He said I was suffering from depression and he strongly advised that I take a low dose antidepressant. He made me listen to him as he carefully described the chemistry of my situation. My much needed serotonin was being 'taken up' in my system too fast because I was grieving, while trying to live each day. The fact that the serotonin was taken up too fast left me exhausted too early in the day. It was true that by 5:00 PM every day, I felt like it was midnight.

Recently I asked Mom, "Did you think I was depressed?"

"I was less worried that you were depressed and more worried that Dave was being mean to you and you had to get out," she replied.

Several months after my vodka-fueled Mother's Day, we did get to the lowest point in our relationship and Mom did advise me to get out. I had been giving Mom a paycheck here and there for her to save for me. Our life was disorganized. Dave was caring for his overly-demanding father during the day and so drunk most evenings, he didn't even notice. My once happy, funny, Donny Osmond-look alike husband was now in so much pain that he had drunk himself into a bitter and belligerent state. Steve would hang out in his room watching the Disney channel in his own little world, for which I was grateful, while I suffered Dave's jibes and jabs, and waited each night for him to pack it in and pass out.

But it was getting to the point where I feared Steve was becoming a shock absorber for the tension in the house. I knew that I couldn't let Dave drag me down with him. I worked too hard—from grief counseling to pharmaceuticals—to survive. I decided to leave and take Steve with me. I had every intention of finding a place nearby and having Steven feel comfortable going back and forth. If we separated, Dave would be on his best behavior with Steve and when we were not there, he could be whatever way he wished. Better, probably, for not having to be around me.

There is a reason the divorce statistic is high for parents who have lost children. You cannot help each other. There was nothing I could do to pull him up and I surely wasn't going to let him pull me down. So our very real breaking point, five months after that Mothers' Day when I worried about his hidden feelings of blame, came in the fall of 2006. I was in my office and feeling so nauseated and dizzy that I needed to lie on the floor while listening to a conference call.

With my cell phone, I dialed my friend at work. "Where are you? I need you to drive me home. I am so sick. I don't even think I can drive. Meet me at the side door."

I packed up and slipped out trying to not to bump into anyone who might talk to me. I slumped in the car and focused on my own breathing. "This is it."

At home, I changed into old sweatpants and my favorite old Cape Cod sweatshirt. I pulled Steven's sleeping bag out of the closet, unrolled it on the couch, and crawled in it. Mom says in retrospect, "You were crawling back into the womb!"

I called Brenda at work. "When Dave comes home, I am telling him I am leaving."

"I told Paul just the other day, 'Get ready, she's done.' Call your mother. Call your mother *right now.* Call me back if you need to, but I really think you need talk to your mother." Brenda was calling in the big guns.

I called my mother at her office.

"You need to get up and go walk and get fresh air before he comes home. Then you can discuss things with a straight head." Mom said. Her boss came in while she was on the phone with me, trying to get her attention. She mouthed, "I'm talking to Kim," and her boss promptly turned around and left her to tend to me. Everyone knew we were at the breaking point.

I did walk around the neighborhood. It was lovely. Beautiful leaves covered the ground. But life was so terrible. *How was I ever going to make it? I have to move out.* On the home stretch, I saw Dave's truck pull in the driveway. It was 1:00 PM and Steven was, thankfully, still at school.

Dave said, "You're home early."

He, too, realized we were at the breaking point. He had been thinking all day. The day before, he was with his father in the backyard building a shed. His niece and her husband stopped by to see it, and his father didn't even say hello to his own granddaughter, he hollered, "less talk, more work!" in his sharp nasal voice. It was a breaking point for Dave too.

"It's over," I said.

"I wish you told me that before I started the shed," he said. Then more seriously, "I know I am mad and angry and mean. Like my old man. And I don't want to be that way. So that is over. If you give me a chance, I'm going to stop being like… him."

It didn't happen overnight, but I did stay. I gave him a chance. I realized he loved me and he was hurting double—for both of us. *Why had this happened to his wonderful son and his best girl? Why had the accident happened to her?* His childhood insecurity resurfaced. He had changed, and so he wondered, *Does she still love me?*

We went to counseling. He admitted he was on a destructive path. I was in the path of his rage. He learned that drinking changed his body chemistry. The drink that once made him relax, was actually putting him on edge. Over time, he found his smile again.

If I have any advice for women, it would be my mother's words of wisdom. Men *really* are *that* stupid. And often, they count on us to know it.

Kim Perone

Making Pies

My dear friend Dawn, Hawaii-Dawn, had given me Patty Griffin's "1000 Kisses" CD, and her song "Making Pies" reminds me of the time after Jack's death. That first Thanksgiving was horrible, only three months later. The holiday season was hitting us head on. We ordered the whole dinner from a caterer and drank red wine all day long. I needed to be sedated. We all did, no doubt.

After 2004, we started going to my sister's house for Thanksgiving. Previously, she had always come home for the holiday, but after we lost Jack, we would pile into her house and live communally from Wednesday through Sunday.

My mother has annual pictures of me napping on the love seat. "There's Kim in 2005, 2006, 2007..."

We would make pies and cook Thanksgiving dinner. The girls would shop on Black Friday and the guys would find something to do. We could not be more comfortable in anyone else's home, and during the Thanksgiving holiday, my sister's house became a haven of comfort.

Last year was another horrible Thanksgiving. Making pies, just the two of us, Mom and me. We did go to my sister's, but she was not with us. *Not in person anyway.* But we were there with Omar and Owen and it was important. No need for to-fur-key (tofu turkey) for Kristen. In fact, we didn't even have turkey at all; we made steak and crab legs. Our anti-Thanksgiving Thanksgiving.

This year, when we realized that Omar and Owen were going to his sister's house in North Carolina to be with his parents, we felt momentary shock and a further sense of loss. Mom learned this through Facebook and called me right away. How incredibly modern!

There is absolutely nothing wrong with Omar going to see his parents. We respect his need to share holiday time, but the change means we will not be together at their house for Thanksgiving, which also coincides with Kristen's birthday.

I love my mother and felt her pain. *A mother's pain. A change. The times are going to change. Someday there will be a new wife; a new mom for Owen. What if she doesn't want us around? Why would she want us around? How will our lives change? Will we drift apart? We can't lose Owen!*

My mother is so strong. She went through all of the scenarios of additional loss and came right back to the present. *Omar has been good to us. He knows we love Owen and he wants us to be involved. He enjoys our company.* We are not worriers, but we are thinkers. Thinking and grief lead you to what I call "ficture"—a picture of the future that is fiction. We cannot know what time will bring, but we still let it strike fear in our hearts.

My stepfather, Dan, talked to Mom and calmed her. He said if Omar becomes involved with someone new this will *increase* our time with Owen, as he will need us as babysitters during his new courtship. Over time perhaps Omar will see us as *his* family, rather than his deceased wife's family. His family is extremely small, limited to his immediate family with no extended family at all. Omar needs his family. But he also needs the kind of family we are, whatever that means. Maybe it means that our schedules never take precedence over Owen. Luckily, we are able to make that true.

Kim Perone

Owen absolutely comes first and always will.

So what to do about Thanksgiving? On comes the cartoon light bulb above my head. I'll just ask Omar if we can still go there for Thanksgiving, even while he is gone, so that we might transition! We will have Thanksgiving, there, just minus Omar, Owen, and of course Kristen, and when Owen and Omar come back Friday night, we'll have a nice weekend together. Phew!

I left Mom a voice mail and sent an email to tell her of my plan. We can't be knocked down. Even if Omar is not there, we can go! Problem solved. *I love you Kristen. I even dreamt of you the other day. I woke up and remembered seeing you and saying "I.... miss...you."*

Mom called back a few days later. "I got your message. Thanks, but, I'm over it," she said simply.

I should not be surprised. It just took that trip back to the "ficture", complete with all of its worry, to return us to today and our present reality. We will have Thanksgiving here, at home, and go to Connecticut for the weekend. It is okay to change. Her steely resolve shows through yet again. My one-tenth of that resolve serves me well. That's something to be thankful for this year.

Maybe, we thought, this shores us up for Christmas. Even better! But a few weeks later, my brother-in-law mentioned that his parents are coming up from Florida for the week of Christmas, which inhibits him from traveling to New York to spend Christmas with us. He assured me that he mentioned to his parents that we would be around, coming to Connecticut sometime the week of Christmas. I took comfort knowing that he understands the delicate situation without me even mentioning it.

I should be the one to pass this news on to Mom. She had

asked me to subtly bring up Christmas to get a feel for what was on his mind. So when I told her, I could hear her disappointment on the phone. I empathized.

"Listen, it is early," I said. "Anything can change."

"Yeah," Mom said in a desperate whisper.

"One twisted ankle or something like that and they will not want to travel up from Florida."

"I do have a voodoo doll. I think I actually got it with Kristen when she was working in Louisiana." I could hear the gears in her mind turning and remembering.

"Authentic! Does it look like anyone in particular yet?" I said.

"Oh, I couldn't do that. Can we just pray for diarrhea of something?" mom pleaded.

"Gonorrhea! Mom, don't you think that is a little harsh?"

I made mom laugh. We needed a joke, a laugh, a lightening of the situation. We needed to be honest in our disappointment. Humor is necessary to keep us off the dark road that leads to self-pity. There's nothing like a good hearty laugh about fake gonorrhea.

Kim Perone

The Plots Thicken

Mom likes to arrange things. Like many people, it keeps her mind busy and focused on the future. Mom's arrangements range from the excitement of plotting her next vacation, to the fun of planning interim short trips to New York City, to the practical aspects of making her own funeral arrangements. She leaves nothing to chance. Her arrangements for trips result in itineraries which are exquisitely detailed and include multiple alphabetical scenarios— A, B, and C—based on any number of events that might veer from the proposed schedule, such as the weather or arrival times.

"If Kristen makes it to Grand Central Station on time," she would say, "she'll meet us at 10:45 but if not, she will meet us at the Blue Grille for lunch at noon," and so on. Kristen's name would appear in columns A, B, and C.

Her arrangements for life now include the afterlife—multiple burial plots in two different states. It all started innocently enough with Grammy's death in 1995. Mom used part of the inheritance to pre-pay a package of her own arrangements. "You will never have to worry about what I would want, it is all done. Just go to Bond's Funeral Home and they will know what to do."

I have been promoted to eulogist since writing this book. After reviewing various chapters she wrote, "You certainly have a way with words. I have full trust in you that you'll have something wonderful, moving, and funny to say at my funeral (date/time still to be determined)." And you just know there's a partial eulogy written in a folder in her filing cabinet. Okay, at least an outline.

The arrangements include two cemetery plots, one for Mom and the other for a potential future spouse or significant other. That was the first set of many plots. Being single, yet optimistic, Mom chose two spots next to Grammy.

Nine years later, we tragically lost Jack. As Mom and I made Jack's arrangements, she (along with the funeral director) had the foresight to direct me to purchase cemetery plots for Dave and me. We will obviously be buried by our son. No need to buy Steven's as he will make these arrangements with his wife long in the future, God willing. Mom decided after this process that Grammy would understand being abandoned so that she could be next to Jack instead of her mother. So she traded the two plots near her mother for two plots near Jack and eventually us.

"I was basically saying bye to Grammy and 'I know you'll understand why I have to leave you with strangers at your side. I have to be with Jack'," my mother explained. "When I swapped my plots next to Grammy for two near Jack, I couldn't completely surround him. I had two, which I put one over his *head* and one at his *feet*. When I realized there was an empty grave next to him I ran straight away to the sellers of the plots to buy the one next to Jack. So now I could rest (while still living) knowing that Jack would be surrounded by family. Who they would be was still to be determined. I planned to be at his side while you or Dave would be at his other side. Who would be at the top and bottom would be a surprise to us all."

I believe this makes three plots. Now enter Dan into the picture. Although he plans on being cremated she figures she needs to buy another plot, *next* to her. That makes four. Now, there are two plots above Jack's grave, one to the side and one below. These strategic moves block Jack in with loved ones to the best of Mom's ability.

It was as if she was buying all of orange on the Monopoly board—St. James Place, Tennessee Avenue, and New York Avenue and then started on green. She's a plot mogul.

Now, I am sure you know where I am going with the next Monopoly move. After Kristen's death, she accompanied Omar, helping him through the arrangements in Connecticut. She gently and awkwardly mentioned that maybe Omar should buy three plots. He didn't understand.

"For Owen?" he asked.

"No honey, you will get married again in the future and shouldn't have to decide which wife to be buried with," Mom gently replied.

In his grief, he naturally said he would not be getting married again. He bought two plots.

"Because I could not be sure of where he would be buried I went back to the cemetery manager the next day and asked about availability in the vicinity of Kristen," she told me. "As luck would have it, there was a double right below, at her feet. It was like a sign. The area seemed to be filling up fast, by all the X's on the plot map, and just by chance the double right below her was available. Chance? I think not. *Someone* had a plan. I had to act fast to stake my claim. So there I was, buying a double plot in the state of Connecticut (at Kris's feet which is where I should be). So now I own four cemetery plots where I really only need one. In the end, I will have a very tough decision about where I want my final resting place. I will have to give you some guidelines, so you will be able to make the decision if I cannot."

In the Connecticut cemetery, they have different places for singles, and doubles/triples. Therefore Mom could not be near Kristen (and perhaps theoretically someday Omar) without buying a double, which she did.

"So to be near her, I had to buy a double plot. Sounds like discrimination. The singles can't mingle with the doubles/triples...?"

Realizing the obvious, that she is a little overloaded with plots, she sold two of her four New York plots to a friend and her husband. Gail and Don will find their final resting place above my head.

Neither my head nor my feet will be there for many reasons, either because I am not there yet or my head or feet have disintegrated. I can assure you I won't be there. None of us are there, in the dirt. It is our marker at the end of life and that is all. I can't use the expression "Roll over in her grave" anymore. I truly cannot. Between Jack and Kristen, I cannot refer to the deceased in a way that implies they are in the grave. I often express Kristen's imagined happiness or approval, but when it comes to disapproval I simply *cannot* say she will "roll over in her grave." Maybe I should say she is "rolling her eyes in heaven."

X Marks the Spot

My father in-law, rest his soul, always liked my mom. He was an old bust-your-chops Italian and she is a firecracker. He loved that she would have a drink with him at our family get-togethers. He'd have his whisky and hand her a glass of wine. Now, drinking was not a hard thing for Mom to do, of course, but he admired her fiery personality and how she would jump right in with the crowd.

Christmas is a big family holiday, held in Auntie Anne's ranch-style house with a finished basement, complete with bar and second full kitchen. This is common for the older Italians. When you have lots of relatives and a small house, what else can you do besides finish your basement?

Uncle Walt had an electric toilet installed downstairs and he would watch carefully as guests went in and out of that particular room making sure they flushed the toilet right. If you didn't hold the lever long enough he would chase you down and bring you back into the bathroom with him to demonstrate the correct operation of the unit.

"Oh, that's how it works. Thanks, Uncle Walt," we would say, mortified as we watched the urine in the bowl go down, down, down.

The first year I went to Auntie Anne's with Dave, we stopped at my parents' house first for morning presents. Kristen was a senior in high school and I had my own apartment. Dave and I had been dating for about three months, and we both knew it was getting serious. After leaving my parents' house, we headed up to Auntie Anne's house, only ten minutes away. We entered the house, which was eerily quiet. The high-end furniture had been lovingly protected in plastic for many years, only recently uncovered and looking brand new. A huge console television stared out at us from the far wall. We put our coats over the back of the couch; the huge pile was the only indication that a party was going on somewhere in the vicinity.

We set off down the stairs. In the basement, a lively party met us. There were hugs and kisses and introductions all around. Dave's cousin Walt manned the bar. Someone brought down a cooler with a bag of ice in it. When putting it down a piece of ice fell out onto the carpet. I promptly picked it up and slipped it into the cooler, under the plastic bag containing the ice.

My future father-in-law saw me do this and yelled at me, "What are you, stupid?! Don't put that in there!"

I could feel my shock rise up and turn red under my skin. My throat choked up and I blinked back tears, reacting to having someone I didn't know yell at me on Christmas in front of a crowd of people. "I put the ice cube in *under* the plastic, I just didn't want it to melt on the rug," I said, somewhat indignantly.

"Well, don't do that. That ice is for the drinks, is all." And he walked away.

When I mentioned it to Dave, he said, "That? That was nothing! If he yelled at you, he likes you."

I was used to a father who never yelled, one who definitely didn't ask me if I was stupid!

After a few years, I became used to my father-in-law. Each Christmas we went to Auntie Anne's basement and had a full sit-down dinner with turkey, ham, and lasagna. The pool table was converted to a snack and dessert table. My little boys used to sit under it and play with their toy cars or Legos. It was a good place for them to be, out of the way of all the stampeding adults. Perhaps (I hope) there was even some fresh air under there. Three quarters of the family smoked. The whole basement was a haze of cigarette smoke, and poor Auntie Anne and Uncle Walt were among the nonsmoking minority. No wonder everyone got pushed to the basement!

About seven years ago, I was wondering if it was time to offer Auntie Anne an 'out.' Everyone started complaining about going there. "The lasagna tastes frozen. She makes it too early..." and other miscellaneous complaints. I felt for her. She does all this work and is nearly eighty years old! Who, might I ask, has *ever* offered to take this chore off of her hands? No one, I bet. My guess was she got stuck with the responsibility, being the oldest child and only daughter in a traditional Italian family. I know what it is like to be a firstborn.

I talked to my niece, Cheryl, to get her thoughts on a change of venue. "Uncle Dave and I would take this over if it is getting too much for Auntie Anne. Do you think it is? Everyone is starting to complain that they don't want to go there, but we've never asked if she'd like to 'pass the baton.'"

Cheryl agreed that we should talk to her.

Our visit with Auntie Anne was delightful. We realized she was becoming a bit senile, but she was telling us stories of her childhood and we were thoroughly enjoying it. "Christmas started originally with just my parents. Wally was just born and I asked my parents to come here. Year after year, we hosted Christmas dinner, then my brothers started coming with their wives, then their kids, and now their kids' kids," she said looking off toward the window with a smile remembering the good old days. "In fact, I have been doing Christmas dinner for fifty-two years!"

Wow, I thought. *The offer to host Christmas dinner is either going to be very flattering for her or highly insulting. I hope we are doing the right thing.* But she seemed to understand and appreciate our gesture.

The next time Mom and I got together with Kristen, I filled them in. Mom had always hosted a huge Christmas Eve party for both sides of our family. It was so much fun for us as kids. I thought of this as I envisioned holding the family Christmas at my house. It is sort of like keeping a tradition, but with different people. Mom didn't mind. In fact, I think she was proud that I would take the lead on Christmas for my in-laws.

When I told her about my conversation with Auntie Anne, and how she reminisced, I added, "She told us she has been doing this dinner for fifty-two years!" making a face like, *eeeek, I hope I did the right thing.*

She slapped me on the back and said, "Just think Kim, after this year, you'll only have fifty-one more to go!" She and Kristen broke into laughter. Kris would never have fallen into this trap!

Christmas involves approximately twenty-five people sitting together at three to four consecutive six-foot tables. In my house, this means moving furniture. My father-in-law was adamant that it is one day, and everyone sits down for dinner *together.* It is not a buffet or cocktail party.

Apparently, X marks the spot for Christmas and it was going

to be my house, from now on, forever and ever, and ever, and ever until some great niece of mine offers to take it off my hands as I drift into senility.

I secretly cursed my mother for making me so responsible. She is a hard act to follow.

Kim Perone

All Clad v the All Pad

On December 23, 2010 I was about as discontented a person could be. I told myself that I was just feeling this way so I could get all of my sadness and angry thoughts out before Christmas hosting duties. This was my grief wave. I was sad that Kristen wasn't alive, that because she was not alive my brother-in-law and Owen were not able to come to see us, and that my son would not have his brother to joke around with and open up presents with on Christmas morning. I was just mad and sad and most of the day I was occupied drying my leaking eyes.

A week prior I had laser eye surgery. So for a week my eyes did, in fact, leak, but this was different. My eyes were better; my heart had issues. After my eye surgery I was a little traumatized. It is fantastic to be able to see clearly, but the tenderness in your eyeballs leaves you feeling very fragile. I rested my eyes and lie in bed after Dave drove me home from the procedure. I told him to give me the phone.

"Hello."

"Hi Mom, it's Kim."

"Oh, hi, honey!"

"I just had laser eye surgery."

"Wow, you *did* end up doing that! Good for you. I tried that, but they said my eye sight wasn't bad enough and they wouldn't let me." Mom has a laundry list of top procedures she wants done.

"It was a little disconcerting."

"What do you mean? I know tons of people who did it and came back to work the next day. They love it."

"I guess because they work on your eyes, and now they are sore and feel traumatized, I feel traumatized."

The procedure involves holding open your eyelids and pulling back your cornea. My eyelids feel like they were rendered helpless to save my eyeballs from the evil alien prodding. I was nervous and scared. I needed to call my mommy!

I needed to hear my mother's reassuring voice.

"It'll be great. I'll have to ask Ellen how she felt right after the surgery. I have never heard anyone say it was hard."

We discussed our Christmas plans and then I took a nap.

But a week later on December 23rd, my heart was dragging me down. I was feeling sorry for myself. Dave was doing some pre-Christmas preparation in the kitchen and he said, "It's not the Christmas you want, that's why." I shrugged. He grocery shops for Christmas each year, because he has free time because of his seasonal business and I am usually working at the office. I was glad he was still up to the task. I certainly wasn't. The closer the holiday came, the slower I moved. I puttered around cleaning and began telling myself, *Ah, it's fine. Good enough. Who cares?* Dave on the other hand speeds up, thank goodness.

On Christmas Eve we host a cocktail party for my side of the family. A few years back we re-combined Mom and Dad due to Kristen's engagement and the need for Kris and Omar to fly to Florida on Christmas day to see his parents. Before that we had separate Dad's side, in-law side, and Mom's side parties. We would hold three parties within a 24-hour period. It was busy, fun, crazy, and festive.

So now, in 2010, we still have Mom and Dad combined for Christmas Eve and that works well. Maybe not perfectly for them, but each of their relatives appreciate seeing the other side. My cousin Joe likes to see my dad. My Aunt Linda enjoys catching up with my mother. They used to see them every Christmas years ago. So it still works for now.

In the flurry of wrapping paper and conversation (and wine), I never feel like I express sufficient appreciation for the gifts. I actually feel guilty each year on Christmas day. Rena gave me a beautiful work of art – she returned the pizza peel (like a big spatula) that Stevie made in wood shop, on which she painted a bottle of wine that says Perone, cheese and grapes, and a brick background. It is gorgeous. We did a lot of ooohing and ahhhing over that. But in all the chaos, I forgot to open the gigantic box sitting in the middle of my living room floor from Mom. The next morning I called my mom. "Merry Christmas. I am sorry I didn't open your present!"

"I wasn't sure if you forgot it or were trying not to open it in front of everyone," she said. "Why that would be, I wasn't sure."

"Sorry, I just knew what it was and then started crashing around midnight. In my rush to get Steve's presents set I totally forgot it. I went to bed when you and everyone left. Dave stayed up and stoked the fire, talking to Rena and Dad."

I had asked Dad and Rena if they wanted to stay overnight in case the weather was bad or they didn't want to drive after a couple of cocktails.

My forgetful behavior, although subconscious, was probably prompted by the fact that the gigantic box contained something very expensive that I did not want. Mom and I had talked on the phone a couple of months earlier and she told me what she was set on buying me for Christmas. I reluctantly told her that we don't really like those...that I don't really need them...they don't wash well...

My mother had purchased a $500.00 set of All Clad pots and pans for me —*or for my kitchen, rather.*

"Well I got them for Kristen for her wedding. Then you guys got them for me. Didn't you get them for Rena the next?"

"Yeah. But we like Teflon. It just seems like you have to use too much oil without it. Dave really doesn't like that. Not that he cooks all the time, but..." we really aren't high end people. Our tastes aren't meant for it. I'm going to have to hear Dave make fun of them forever, forever.

She hadn't bought the set yet. "Well, this is what I want you to have."

"Oh, okay." I could tell that was that.

"It is for your kitchen. Your new kitchen *deserves* it." Mom has spoken.

Three weeks later, I still needed to wash them and put them in the cabinet, moving the pots and pans that work perfectly well out of the way and what then? The garage? (more complaining from Dave) Throw them out? (What a waste.) The box is in the spare room, where we pile all the clean laundry. I keep looking at it and thinking, *"...that All Clad could be an iPad!"* Not that she should spend that much money, I don't want her to. But if she is going to, it should be something revolutionary and electronic.

I must get that from Dad.

Kim Perone

In Her Shoes

When I was little, I would don my mother's silver heels, her pink negligee with purple trim, and its matching robe. I would dance and swirl around the house. The negligee set was beautiful and long and it wafted in flowing waves. I wondered how old I would be when my feet would actually fit into those silver shoes. They were exquisite. The simple pumps, shimmering silver pleather, with heels neither too high or too low, were just right for me. I was a little aspiring actress, who clomped around the living room with all the grace of a five year old.

Mom was going to have a baby soon. I loved my baby dolls and was very eager to have a real one in the house. I would be the best helper *ever*, because I was a big girl. I was starting kindergarten in the fall.

Back in the spring, I was the one who got to tell Dad that Mom was pregnant when we came back from the doctor's office. I was ecstatic! She looked sad, but she was just surprised. That episode with the flu must have interfered with the effectiveness of the birth control pill. Mom said she hadn't yet forgotten the difficulty of my birth.

Kristen's birth was totally opposite of mine.

"She was born in forty-five minutes, and practically fell out!" mom said, whereas I refused to make my entrance. After thirty hours of labor, I think they broke down and used forceps to pull me out. As adults, my sister and I joked that it was because I had a big head and she had a little one, which was actually true.

My parents were still young. My mother was eighteen when I was born. So when she was pregnant with Kristen, she was barely twenty-three years old.

Once the surprise wore off and reality set in, they were happy. After all, I was already five. If it was a baby boy, he was going to be Robert Jr. and if it was a baby girl she would be Kristy.

During my mother's pregnancy there was a very popular detective show Christy Love, also the name of the main character. According to my mother, it totally ruined the name Kristy for her, she was looking for different and it had become popular. By the time Kristen was born, she would be called just Kris, Kris-ten or maybe Kris-sy. She was a gorgeous baby with jet black hair and a button nose and I was a proud big sister. When Kristen was fussy, which was often, I walked her up and down the hall of our trailer in her umbrella stroller.

Our personalities were different as well. Kristen was a cranky, colicky baby, so much so that when she was an adult and stories about her came up, she would say, "Yes, I was a terrible baby...." I, on the other hand, was a singer, dancer, and all-around entertainer who, as a baby, slept all the time. In reality, I think Kristen was extremely stressed in the womb. My mother's pregnancy was eventful and worrisome.

Late in the summer, the beginning of my mother's final trimester, my father was diagnosed with a brain tumor. The tumor obviously needed to be removed and biopsied to determine whether it was malignant or benign. He was promptly scheduled for surgery at Lenox Hospital. I was shuffled back and forth to friends' houses, while Mom and Dad went back and forth to New York City for tests and the operation. Although benign, the brain surgery at age twenty-four was scary for both of them.

My father's tumor was removed and there were relatively minor, yet permanent, injuries. His right eye would not close all the way ever again, his mouth was crooked due to the pulling of tendons and he was now completely deaf in his right ear. They also told him he would be unable to stand on one foot with his eyes closed, due to some inner ear damage. All of this was manageable.

Nevertheless, I think my sister was jostled and jolted during her time in the womb. My mother was anxious and worried. *What if he dies? What if I become a widow? What if it comes back?*

A couple months later Kristen Marie was born, giving us a happier hospital experience. We recently looked at some old picture slides and there was my mom in the hospital bed with 6 lbs. 12 oz. and 22-inch baby girl in her arms.

Kindergarten was great fun and I ran home each day excited to see Mom and my baby sister. I even brought home chicken pox and gave it to my sister. Our pediatrician, Dr. Nitchman, came to the house. I remember having to drink that awful pink syrup, but the upside was eating all of those butterscotch candies and getting to sleep on the couch. There are black-and-white photos of this time that are overexposed (Dad was developing his own photos). My face was bright white and blurry, but you could see the dot marks on my face. There were pictures of Mom too, looking exhausted.

Dad had an uncanny way of calming my colicky sister. Every day after he came home from working as an electrician at various construction sites in town, Mom would give her over to him and she would fall asleep on his chest as they lay on the couch.

A cute little family, we were happy and felt loved. It couldn't have been easy for Mom and Dad, but they were strong, determined, and young enough to handle having very little. My father worked two jobs and went to college full-time after I was born. There is a picture of me on his shoulders at his community college graduation.

Mom was extremely talented with household crafts. She sewed us matching outfits and matching nightgowns for all our baby dolls. She even made Barbie doll clothes! People always thought my mother must be my sister. She looked even younger than she was with her long blond hair, parted in the middle in classic '70s style. She had a burst of freckles on her nose and cheeks and a sweet smile.

From the time Kristen was born we girls had outnumbered Dad three to one, but he didn't mind one bit. He loved all his girls and we loved him. We spent the next twenty years uneventfully, or so it seemed.

So I danced in mom's shoes then and I dance in Kristen's now. After she passed away in September of 2009, I took most of her shoes. We have the same size foot. I even took some socks. When I wear them, I feel close to her. Mom and I both have items of hers we wear. Mom has a pair of sneakers. Her foot is two sizes smaller than ours, but it works with heavy socks.

It is hard to believe Kristen is gone before us. That wasn't the natural order. We do comfort each other, but every time I call and say, "Hi Mom. It's Kim," I want to kick myself. I am the only woman calling her Mom these days. I cringe the minute the words are out of my mouth.

Maybe someday we'll have granddaughters we can let clomp around in our shoes.

Speed, Sex, and Sensitive Subjects

Best to talk about the birds and the bees when in a car going 55 miles per hour," says Mom. "Teenagers never want to talk to you so you have to get them when they can't get away from you."

Now that I have a fourteen-year-old son, I realize how very true that is.

As I mentioned previously, Mom wanted to make sure we knew what was what. She wanted us to know how you got pregnant, a piece of information she was unsure of until she was *actually* pregnant.

Not us. I remember being in the car with Mom, with a friend of mine when we were sixteen. Looking forward at the road, Mom said, "It will take years before it is good." She made the word years sound very long.

Her note on semen, "What goes up must come down."

But I will never, ever forget cleaning one day when I was seventeen (a rare day, not sure why) and I was putting clean clothes away. I went to put underwear in mom's drawer and as I slipped the skivvies in, I found a box of condoms. I must admit, my memory is fuzzy on this, but I think the box *was* in a brown paper bag. I guess curiosity got the best of me.

Yuck! My parents have sex!

Don't we all feel that way about our parents? Dave thinks I am a little overly concerned now that Steve is fourteen, but I say "You can't un-ring that bell!" *If our kid hears or God forbid barges in on us, we'll never get our images off of his burned retinas!* Ugh.

Last summer when we were all in Michigan for a baseball tournament, when the boys (Steve and his friend Joe who stayed with us) were out of the room, Dave was getting frisky.

"No, no, no," I said. "There is nothing sexy about being in a hotel with your child and thirteen of his teenage friends and their parents." Oh, and some younger siblings too. *Am I crazy?*

Well, I didn't think so, until I was talking to the other moms. The one said, "Sure, every day when the kids go off to breakfast," then she made a hand-clapping movement, like bingo bango bongo. "Stan thinks it is the best vacation *ever*. Sex and baseball every day!" We all laugh heartily.

Then another one said she and her husband snuck out and did it in the bushes outside the hotel! She said they felt like teenagers again. If I felt like a teenager again, it would have nothing to do with sex. I just think *my poor husband*. Have I ever felt sexy?

Nowadays, I see mothers taking their teenage daughters to Victoria's Secret. My mother bought me granny panties and flannel nightgowns. I definitely think my mojo was stunted by my parents' paranoia of teen pregnancy. I don't blame them. For them, I think it was subconscious. Like that time after the band concert.

As a flutist I was front row, on stage. Our music teacher was adamant that we never cross our legs while playing an instrument. It interferes with your diaphragm and air and whatnot.

Well, that is not a good thing when you are in a skirt on a stage that is raised five feet. My mother had a fit. I didn't even see it coming. I was just hopping down from the stage, ready to go for

Kim Perone

ice cream after the concert. Once in the car, she said "Your legs were open and we could see everything!" I was mortified for days and days. I didn't want to go back to school ever.

Now, I am forty-one and thinking, "*What everything?*" My knees couldn't have been more than four inches apart. I had underwear on. I was in the fifth grade. The nearest audience member was thirty feet from me! Past the orchestra pit area! I bet if I mentioned this, Mom wouldn't even remember this incident that is still so vivid for me. I really believe this was a subconscious affront to my mother, a fear of my growing up, and a lesson in sexuality.

In the early days of our relationship, Dave would tell me to relax. To which I admitted it is hard to relax, because sex is so "un-lady-like." Good God, it is amazing he kept dating me. I needed therapy!

Well that was twenty years ago now.

So, just when I was starting to come into my own as a sexual being at thirty-five, we tragically lost our son Jack and my life started feeling unsexy, very sad, and out of control. Then there was my nervous breakdown two years later, when I couldn't carry the pain and dysfunction anymore that led me to antidepressants. These helped tremendously for focus, stability, and emotional control, but it dropped my libido into Never-never Land. So at my sexual peak, I feel like I would rather read a good book than have sex.

Now that six years has passed since Jack's death and one year since Kristen's, our life is more normal and stable, I am working my way off of these antidepressants. Being in your forties and not wanting sex is more depressing than anything else at this point. Living is all I have left.

I can do it. I want to feel again. I want to emote. I want to learn how to be sexy. I want that bubbling up feeling that makes you grab your husband and have a thrashing crashing good Hollywood moment.

Let's face it; I want to be able to keep up with the other baseball moms.

Kim Perone

Dreams

I am typing George Clooney's autobiography on cookie dough. Chocolate chips poke up through the space between words. I note how down to earth he is; how nice it is to be around him. Oops, a typo. I was distracted while listening to his calm deep voice and gazing longingly at his salt and pepper hair. *Backspace backspace backspace ...*

Isn't that just like dreams? What the heck? My dreams almost never make sense!

But my mother says her dreams always make sense. My mother dreams of flying. In her dreams, she flies over everything.

"Seriously?" I ask her. People talk about falling and running, but my mother speaks of flying. I think this is because she is a woman with big dreams. She thinks big, has big ideas, big plans, big everything. If you are going to do it, do it to the nth degree. That is Mom.

A by-product of that need for big is that these *big* things tend to be complicated. The big things make big work and I am often dragged into it. Like Thanksgiving—there needs to be forty-five side dishes. I exaggerate, there are really only forty. Pearled onions and peas, squash, brandy-marinated cranberries, chardonnay gravy, bourbon mashed potatoes (hey, there's a theme here) I could go on and on and on. No one likes these except Mom. The rest of us just love mashed potatoes, cranberry sauce out of a can sliced where the can molded bumps along the side. But it just isn't Thanksgiving for Mom if these side dishes are not there. So we spend hours and hours making a meal that is eaten several hours late and digested fifteen minutes later. Mom sits down around the fourteenth minute. We generally clean up around her full dinner plate. We should just wait, but she can't really sit long either so she pops up right along with us. But why is this how mom does things? Why?

This is the way Mom does things because Mom likes the picture more than the activity. She wants to create a perfect picture and she takes a great deal of pride in a job well done. And she always has. The table looks lovely with all those side dishes that create a color palette of yellows, greens, and burgundy—the colors of the holiday. When I was young, my mother made twenty kinds of Christmas cookies and arranged them on a plate that was more beautiful than anything any caterer has ever done. My sister and I walked to our neighbors' houses handing out mini versions of the original masterpiece that would sit on our dining-room table waiting for our guests to arrive on Christmas Eve.

When Jack was born, she took my 'blankie' which I had carried around for five years, and cut it into two and used it to make a teddy bear for him. Then when Steven was born she did the same for him with the other half. She said not to have more kids because she didn't do thirds of the blanket!

More moments for peak creativity were awaiting mom. Weddings make perfect events for a beautiful picture. My mother made my sister's wedding cake. She said the stress may have taken a few years off her life, because it was not just the cake, but also the veil, her dress jacket, the decorations, and all of the flowers from bouquets to table arrangements. But it was worth it. She calmed herself during the process by saying (specifically of the cake) if anything

Kim Perone

goes wrong it will be a wedding memory.

A couple years later, my nephew Owen's christening was the stage for another picture-perfect performance. This was Mom's first experience with fondant. She spent the entire day working on the top of the cake. Talk about "the icing on the cake"! In case you aren't familiar with it, fondant is frosting no one eats. It is like clay. She made a sculpture of a baby who had a real body, peach skin and all, even a button nose. To top it all off the fondant baby was nestled in a tiny fondant bassinet and covered with a fondant blanket covering bare frosting feet! This creation sat atop a cake that looked like a field of white daisies.

Are you tired yet? It tires me out just watching her! But for my mom the awe and applause make it all worth it. Actually, the reward is hers. She is incredibly talented. She is a dynamo, and dynamos need to stretch their wings and do big things. I guess they need to fly in life as well as in their dreams. So when it comes to my dreams—not the sleeping kind, but my real dreams, my true life goals or desires—I *do* believe they are possible. Because with Mom, I always saw the ideas take flight. I always took that for granted before now.

Kim Perone

Almost Famous

My mother gets a kick out of celebrity mothers who say, "I always knew he would be a star."

"I could say that about you," she says.

Alas, I am not a star, but I was always goofing around, singing, dancing and entertaining, which, apparently, celebrities do when they are young. She is pretty entertaining herself, yet also able to build a Hollywood set.

Ever since I shared the concept of this book with my mother, I have stunted her ability to speak offhandedly. I can tell when she is trying to be profound and educational.

Recently she commented on the Diwali party pictures from her office. For the office party, her Indian coworkers brought in saris for other women. "What beautiful outfits! I almost didn't recognize you!" I say because she is the shortest, blondest, whitest woman in all the photos.

She said it was so much fun and the costumes so ornate it was like "falling into a box of crayons." True, but that seemed well thought-out! I laughed.

I would be the same way. Someone is writing a book about the funny things you say. So now what do you say? How do you keep up with the standard you didn't even know you were setting? It is hard to believe that it is the most ordinary things she says, without giving it an ounce of thought, that are the most poignant to me. Her pragmatic nature never ceases to amaze me.

When I mentioned that my friend is experiencing a bit of 'empty nest syndrome,' Mom was surprised.

"Oh, did Ryan move out?" she asked.

"No, but he is an only child and older so he is really independent now and I think that Mary is trying to figure out what to do. You know, what she wants to do, her own thing, hobbies," I reply.

"But empty nest is when the kids move away," she said.

In this moment, in my mother's mind, she cannot make the leap that it may be a feeling rather than a condition of the house. But maybe it is a condition of the house rather than a feeling. She could be right. There are more ways than one to perceive life.

I love this about her, because I am so opposite at times that I drive myself crazy. There is simply no black and white in my life. This makes me a little too accommodating to the world. It makes me unsure of my decisions and leads me to ponder or overanalyze.

Not Mom. Things are practical. And funny. And I am never allowed to forget there is a bright side to everything. Her mind is so fast. She can take any bad situation and turn it into the better version of a worse situation. Jack dies and she is the first to point out "it is a miracle that all three of you didn't die. I saw the car." Kristen dies and she is thankful for the gift that is Owen.

Now *that* is a gift. *We lost them from this earth, but at least we have each other.* And what is left, is never to be minimized. Martyrdom is self-indulgent.

I hope you will forgive me for putting humor side-by-side with loss. Not everyone can go there but for me it was a necessary part of the process. I could not talk about my mother without dealing with our losses.

Kim Perone

Once I started this book, I realized I was documenting a true star. A true character. Move over John Wayne. The more I wrote, the more I realized that mothers and daughters never tire of stories about this ordinary, yet extraordinary relationship. Our mothers mold us whether we conform or rebel. Their words affect us whether they are funny or compelling. Their actions in life can set us up for success by developing a sense of what is possible or probable.

Our relationship makes me long for the daughter I never had. My time has passed to act on that, although Mom says encouragingly, "You have time," while I secretly think of foster parenting.

Outwardly I reply, "Dave doesn't have time!" My husband turned fifty this year.

But maybe, just maybe, there is still time for me to become famous. Still time for Mom to go on talk shows and say how silly I was as a kid, yet with a searing ambition, so much so that she knew I would be famous one day.

And if so, I would *certainly... like to thank my mother ....*

Kim Perone

Drawing Conclusions

Coming to the conclusion of this book was an unbelievable experience for me. I had done it. *If it doesn't go anywhere beyond my dining room table and my hard drive, I am happy,* I thought. I love every one of the 40,000 words.

Why? Because I did it! I wrote a book. I didn't stare at blank pages. I had things to say. I learned that I could wrap up any chapter with a thought, a moral, or a laugh, because it is really there. I could describe the scenes which were the memories in my head. My goal had already been accomplished. Now, if I could publish it, then that is a *dream,* not the goal. The goal had been achieved. *Yay me! Champagne, anyone?*

The book was ready to look real, so I asked my aunt, who is an artist, if she could make a picture of a cartoon-ish woman vacuuming for the cover of my book. I sent her some clip art that matched the concept in my head. She asked me if I was committed to the retro look, which is common in vacuuming images.

"No, glad you asked. Actually it would be better to move away from that. This is a look back into the '70s and '80s, not the '50s," I replied.

"Okay, now that I read the two chapters you sent me, I have ideas," her email read.

The last thing I wanted to do was hem her in creatively. So I left it at that, without further explanation.

When I received her rendition, I could feel the little butterflies jumping around in my stomach. This is it. This is where I was going with this. I like it. I love it!

As a communicator, I believe visualization is an important exercise, so I immediately copied the picture into a mock cover of my own creation. "#1 New _P_ork Times Bestseller" on the top, of course. "A must read." Quoting a very famous author, and literally writing 'very famous author.' Beside myself with excitement, I sent it to Mom.

I called right away. "Did you see it?"

"Yes, I just opened it. It looks just like me!" mom said.

"Um, I think it is me," I reply wincing, remembering that I did talk to her about maybe taking a picture of her all dressed up with a vacuum. "I did send a couple of chapters, and I think Diane took the creative liberty and, well, when I saw it the hair was longer and she was more dressed down... I think it is me."

"But I thought you wanted me on the cover," Mom said.

"I did, but I just let Diane go with the idea and when I saw it...." I drifted off, not really having an answer. I didn't say to Diane, "...make sure it's Mom" or anything like that. And when I saw the picture, I saw a cartoon of myself and liked it, I suppose. _Awkward._

Mom said, "You? But she's vacuuming. _"_

Pay it Forward

Authors Note:

Finalizing the writing of this book was great; finalizing the actual book was torture. I was nervous and anxious. I was afraid and contemplated the reception my story would receive. Early feedback revealed it might be more poignant than hilarious. *Will it bring readers down, more than it lifts them up?* I contemplated the reception I would receive from colleagues and acquaintances. How would this affect my career? Would family members feel like I was sharing Jack and Kristen with strangers without their consent? I began to wonder why I was subjecting my soul to such scrutiny. A friend and original editor said "You bled this." And I did. He added "It's like looking into your soul." Rereading it over and over during the editing process reminded me that was true.

On the home stretch - publishing - there was still time for me to turn back, pack it neatly on a shelf and feel a sense family history recorded.

Then I remembered that this wasn't even my first vacuum book. I ran to the bins where I keep Jack's things and there it was – a dusty three ring binder with laminated pages. A child's vacuum book. Like many two-year-olds, Jack was equally enamored with and terrified of the vacuum. The poem in beginning is my first vacuum book. This is my second. It helped me reflect on why it was important to publish this book.

When we lost Jack, I lived on a steady diet of books about the

horrors of life, resilience of its survivors, and significant loss. I
still do, just not as specifically or regularly. Those books were the
oxygen in my lungs. The first of these books arrived in the mail
from a business acquaintance, it was given to her at church one
Sunday and she promptly mailed it to me with a note, *"...I thought
you could use this. Thinking of you with love, Sally"*

The book was <u>Treasures from the Dark</u>, by Dwight Reighard.
This led to many others, including <u>A Grace Disguised</u>, Gerald Sitt-
ser, <u>After the Darkest Hour the Sun Will Shine Again</u>, by Elizabeth
Mehren, and <u>I'd Rather Laugh</u>, by Linda Richman. At the time,
I sternly told myself, if they lived through the loss of children,
spouses, and mothers – some at the same time - I must too. I
learned I wasn't alone.

To bring this book into the world, I reminded myself of those
who are suffering who could use the lift, the lesson, the laugh, and
the support. It is important to me that they know that *they are not
alone.*

When you see me smiling in the photo on the back cover, taken
by my son with a cheap digital camera as I stood in my driveway saying goodbye to my father who had stopped by after work, may you
gain a sense that it is possible to smile and laugh again. It is. You will.
If someone you know thinks they won't, they can, they will.

I also survived by leaning on the foundation built by my parents and this book is a compliment to them.

If you have gained any strength from this book, either from
hearing from the survivors of loss or from my mother's wisdom,
I am glad and proud. Pass this book on to someone who needs it
now. If even one single person feels stronger or more able to laugh
at life, then I can rest. This book is aimed at honoring the authors
whose books helped me survive and pay it forward.

Acknowledgements

The author gratefully acknowledges the kindness and support of the following people: my friends, original editors, and champions John and Julie McIntyre, my editor Victoria Wright, two artists who make this book jump off the shelf, my aunt and brilliant artist and cartoonist Diane Rector and graphic designer David Abbott, My Book Sisters, Maria Maynard, MaryEllen Kavanaugh, Jeannie Sawyer, Janice Balch, Nigar Hale, and Colleen Ganey, and my family: my mother and stepfather Claudia and Dan, my father Robert for giving me the emotional intelligence to weave a good story and my stepmother Rena, my brother-in-law Omar and nephew Owen Mureebe, my niece Cheryl Santorelli and aunt Janet McQuade, my inner circle of best friends Brenda and Paul Lukasiewicz and Dave Bancroft who saw us through impossible times, my son Steve for being a great kid, and my first born Jack and only sister Kristen, for their divine inspiration. *Meet me at the Gates!*

My husband Dave, who supported this crazy venture and put up with a messy house even though I wasn't working for pay! (*I'm still your 'little investment.'*) Ann Simpson-MacDowell, an angelic grief counselor at Haven in Schenectady, NY who told me I should write a book, and the Written Art Studio, Albany, NY.

I also thank all the women I met along the way during my year of writing, who asked, "What do you do?" and when I replied "I am writing a funny book about my mother," they each, in their own way, threw me their unbridled support saying they would *love* a book about this special relationship and some actually said "I want a signed copy!" as if I were a celebrity.   Thank you Sisters!

The wall of fame

(Clockwise from top) Ironic! The parents who grounded me indefinitely for smoking at 16, actually took this picture of me a decade earlier; Mom, Kristen and I, 1975; Family Photo 1975; Me in 1975; Camping laundry? Mom always loved to clean. Even outdoors!; Kris and me.

The wall of fame

(Clockwise from top) Nanny and baby Jack all decked out for fourth of July 1995; Jack and Steven 1999; Blankie Teddy, made lovingly by mom for Jack from my childhood tattered blankie. Steve got his a few years later; Mothers' Day 2006, photo by Steven Perone; Family photo at beach in Cape Cod, our annual vacation. People used to look at us the four and say, "Hey, one looks like you and one looks like you!"; Jack, Cape Cod 2002; Mom coaxed back toward her creative and domestic self by making Jack's 5th birthday cake.

The wall of fame

(Clockwise from top) The real elephant in the room; Dad walks Kristen toward her groom on September 23, 2006 past the Peeing Cherub Fountain. Still slimey!; The three of us posing for photo Thanksgiving 2007 at Kristen's house. Kristen was pregnant with Owen. Note I am pushing Mom's wine glass down for the photo. She normally holds it up proudly for photos! (surprise); Dad giving Kristen away at her wedding; Kristen and Owen September 2008;

The wall of fame

(Clockwise from top) Steve, Kristen and I on a trip with mom to NYC in 2006; Dave and me, 2007; Nanny and Owen coloring; Nanny and Owen, October 2010; Luckily, I listened to my gut in July of 2009 and spent an extra week in Connecticut with Kris and Owen, prior to my planned vacation in Connecticut later in August. We did everything that week, including taking Owen to the ocean. When I got back, Mom called me to say she was very sick and in the hospital. That was the beginning of her last six weeks alive. Go with your gut, it is trying to tell you something; Owen at the Beach with butterfly on his arm.

Kim Perone

About the Author

Kim Perone is a communication professional who lives with her husband and son in Saratoga, New York. Kim operates *CommCapabilities,* an independent communications consulting firm and is a writer- for-hire with a focus on documenting personal stories. Vacuum Like No One is Watching is her first book.

www.VacuumLikeNoOneisWatching.com
www.KimPerone.com
www.CommCapabilities.com

www.onepercent-cure.org

ONE% is an organization founded by friends and family of Kristen Marie (Percent) Mureebe who were affected by the love and courage Kris showed during her battle with Ewing's Sarcoma.
Categorized as an "orphan cancer," Ewing's Sarcoma is often overlooked and receives very little research funding. Through ONE%, we hope to raise awareness and funds for research and treatment of this rare type of cancer.
Kris touched our hearts, and it is our goal to extend this love, courage, and support to those affected by this rare cancer.